Christine M. Hand Gonzales, Ed.D.

MY

COMPANION WORKBOOK TO THE COMPREHENSIVE

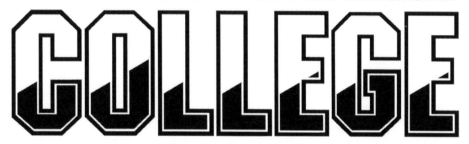
COLLEGE

INTERACTIVE E-BOOK WITH MORE THAN 1,200 LIVE LINKS

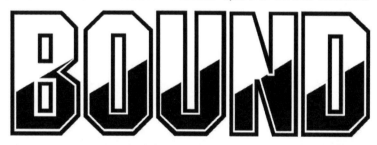
BOUND

TO THE BEST COLLEGE INFORMATION ON THE WEB

COLLEGE BOUND:
Proven Ways to Plan and Prepare
for Getting Into the College
of Your Dreams
by Christine M. Hand Gonzales

PLAN

2013 / 2014 EDITION

College Path, LLC

2390 Wedgefield Rd.

Sumter, South Carolina 29154

Third Edition.

ISBN-13: 978-1491203668
ISBN-10: 1491203668

Author: Christine M. Hand Gonzales, Ed.D.

Design and Production: www.klearIDEA.com

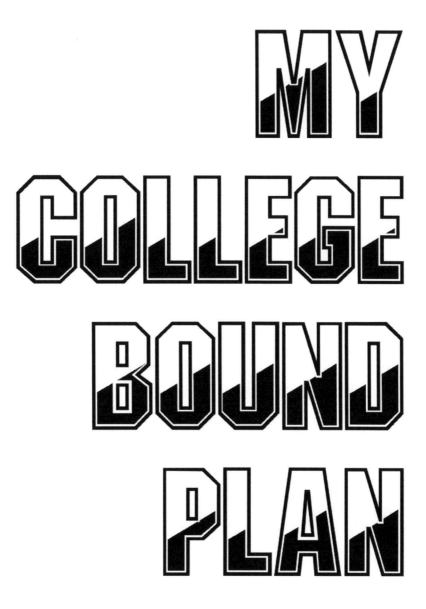

MY COLLEGE BOUND PLAN

THIS PLAN BELONGS TO:

ABOUT THE AUTHOR — "DR. CHRIS"
CHRISTINE M. HAND GONZALES, ED.D.

Dr. Christine Hand Gonzales has over twenty years combined experience as a consultant, instructor, high school college counselor, and registered therapist. Her work with high school juniors and seniors has focused on career exploration and college counseling.

Dr. Hand-Gonzales is a graduate of St. Lawrence University where she received a B.A. in Art Education and Economics. She went on to earn a Master's in Counseling Education from the University of Bridgeport, and a Doctorate in Counseling Psychology from Argosy University. Dr. Gonzales is an instructor for UCLA's online College Counseling Certificate Program.

Other books by Dr. Hand-Gonzales include *COLLEGE BOUND: Proven Ways to Plan and Prepare for Getting into the College of Your Dreams*, *Your College Planning Survival Guide: Smart Tips from Students, Parents, and Professionals Who Made It Through,* and *Paying For College Without Breaking the Bank*.

For more information, visit www.College-Path.com.

Welcome to "My College Bound Plan"

"This workbook is based on the interactive eBook: COLLEGE BOUND: Proven Ways to Plan and Prepare for Getting into the College of Your Dreams. It can be used alone, or with COLLEGE BOUND." – Dr. Chris

Dear Students and Parents,

COLLEGE BOUND: Proven Ways to Plan and Prepare for Getting into the College of Your Dreams, available as an interactive eBook on Amazon.com, is a comprehensive and useful guide for students and parents; providing live links to over 1,200 verified college-related resources including admissions, financial aid, and scholarship resources – organized by topic and college planning timeline. If you do not already have a copy, you can purchase a fully interactive copy from Amazon.com.

My College Bound Plan is designed to act as a companion workbook to use in conjunction with the **COLLEGE BOUND** eBook so you can have all the tools you need as you plan your personal path to college.

As always, I wish you all the very best,

Dr. Chris

Christine M. Hand Gonzales, Ed.D., Author
"Knowledge is Power"

P.S. Follow my college planning blog on Facebook, Twitter and via RSS Feed:

Twitter ID: https://twitter.com/drchristinehand

Friend the College Path Fan Page on Facebook:

http://www.facebook.com/pages/College-Pathcom/74842441589

Subscribe to the College-Path.com RSS Feed: http://feeds.feedburner.com/CollegePath

TABLE OF CONTENTS

I. The Timeline - "Where Do I Start?"

This section includes the worksheets and checklists referred to in Chapter One of COLLEGE BOUND.

"Are you thinking about attending college or training in a field of interest? You can start to position yourself to get into college by using this planning timeline as a guide and checklist and reading the first chapter of the COLLEGE BOUND eBook." – Dr. Chris

THE COLLEGE PLANNING TIMELINE

COLLEGE CHOICE	TESTING/COURSES	APPLICATIONS
MIDDLE SCHOOL YEARS		
☐ Read, read, read. ☐ Get involved in activities.		
FRESHMAN YEAR		
☐ Meet with your counselor to begin talking about careers and college. ☐ Enroll in appropriate college-preparatory courses. ☐ Get good grades because this year will count towards your GPA, and scholarship opportunities will open up to those students who take their coursework seriously. ☐ Explore your interests and extracurricular activities. ☐ Investigate college campuses. You may want to start near your home. ☐ Review college websites. ☐ Investigate summer enrichment programs, volunteer activities, or summer jobs. ☐ Talk with your parents about financing. ☐ Read, read, and read to build vocabulary and comprehension skills. ☐ Practice writing - you will need this skill no matter what.		
SOPHOMORE YEAR – FALL		
☐ See freshman year information above. ☐ Attend PSAT (preliminary SAT) and the PLAN (preliminary ACT test) Review sessions in English class. ☐ Visit colleges when convenient, not to make a decision but to learn. ☐ Thinking about military academies such as Army, Navy, Air Force, or Marines? Start researching now. ☐ Attend College Fairs; become familiar with college entrance requirements. ☐ Build a resume of extracurricular activities, volunteering, and summer jobs and experiences.	☐ Take PSAT as practice. ☐ Take PLAN. ☐ Take SAT Subject Tests if appropriate.	
SOPHOMORE YEAR – WINTER		
☐ Attend Financial Aid Workshop. ☐ Review and register for junior year courses. ☐ Attend College Fairs. ☐ PSAT and PLAN Results Program for students and parents.	☐ Take SAT Subject Tests if appropriate.	

JUNIOR YEAR – FALL AND WINTER

☐ Introduce yourself to your counselor.	☐ Take the PSAT.	
☐ Attend PSAT Review in English class.	☐ Take SAT Reasoning Test if appropriate.	
☐ Attend College Fairs.	☐ Take SAT Subject Tests if appropriate.	
☐ Attend Counselors Workshops for Juniors.		
☐ If the school uses the data management system "Naviance Family Connection," register and complete resume, surveys, and assessments.		
☐ Attend small group sessions.		
☐ Determine college criteria; discuss with parents. Parents should attend Financial Aid Presentation.		
☐ Attend local forums at high school for students and parents.		
☐ Schedule appointment with a counselor to discuss college options.		
☐ Complete student activity profile, and student and parent questionnaires.		
☐ Attend College Fairs in your area.		

JUNIOR YEAR – WINTER – January to February

☐ Meet with counselor.		
☐ Attend PSAT Review session for students and parents with a counselor.		
☐ Plan itinerary for Spring Break college visits.		
☐ Parents should attend Junior Parent Meeting at the school.		
☐ Students should attend college planning workshops at school.		
☐ Decide on courses for senior year.		
☐ Attend area College Fairs: NACAC, the National Association of College Admissions Counseling.		

JUNIOR YEAR – WINTER – January to March

☐ Get on college emailing lists.	☐ Sign up for March and May SAT Reasoning Tests, SAT Subject Test, or ACT with Writing, if needed for college admission.	
☐ Review college guides, and make a primary list of colleges.	☐ Consider the courses required for college and select program for senior year.	
☐ Schedule 50-minute family conference with counselor.		
☐ Develop a resume of activities for college applications and for teachers and counselors who will be writing you a letter of recommendation.		

JUNIOR YEAR – SPRING – March to June

☐ Choose colleges to visit and request information: "view book," application, and financial aid brochures.	☐ June SAT Reasoning Test or SAT Subject Test, ACT with Writing.	☐ Ask teachers to write letters of recommendation.
☐ Athletes: Complete NCAA Eligibility form and turn in transcript request to Athletics Office.	☐ Take AP tests.	☐ Give teachers forms and activity profile unless documents will be transmitted electronically.
☐ Attend Athletic Recruiting Workshop.		☐ Applications usually not available before June.
☐ Refine your activities resume for counselor recommendation.		
☐ Ask teachers for recommendations in the spring if required by the colleges you will be applying to.		
☐ Send thank you notes to college admissions reps after visits.		

JUNIOR YEAR – SUMMER / RISING – June to August

☐ Review college websites, view books, and catalogues.	☐ Prepare for fall - SAT Reasoning Test, SAT Subject Tests and ACT with Writing.	☐ Research application process for each college on your list.
☐ Visit colleges.		☐ Initial campus interviews, if appropriate.

☐ Refine college list. ☐ Work on college essays.		☐ Schedule college visits in advance.

JUNIOR YEAR – LATE SUMMER

☐ Plan fall visits and interviews. ☐ Attend Application Workshop set by the high school counselor.		

SENIOR YEAR – FALL – September to November

☐ Follow up with teachers regarding letters of recommendation. ☐ Attend an essay writing workshop in English class. ☐ Meet college reps who come to your school and to local functions. ☐ Visit colleges on two designated weekends. ☐ Schedule local or on-campus college interviews if required. ☐ Attend College Fair in September. ☐ Keep copies of all applications. ☐ October - Turn in Early Admission Applications and Rolling Applications. ☐ Give counselors secondary school report or counselor form for colleges and a request for a transcript to be mailed with list of senior year courses. ☐ Send standardized test scores directly to colleges that request them. ☐ Turn in Regular Applications in early Nov. ☐ ROTC Scholarships, are due by Dec. 1.		☐ Schedule campus interviews if allowed by the college. ☐ Request official transcript form counselor to be mailed to all colleges you are applying to. ☐ Finish essays and complete applications if applying early application method. ☐ Give counselors and teachers your requests for letters of recommendation to be emailed electronically or via mail. ☐ Begin researching and applying for scholarships. ☐ Check early action application deadlines due mid-September. ☐ Applications for rolling decision; early action and early decision the beginning of October. ☐ Regular applications due first week of November. ☐ Complete CSS Profile from College Board, if needed by college to make an early estimate of aid in November.

SENIOR YEAR – WINTER – December to January

☐ Look for scholarships and complete forms. ☐ Attend "Transitions to College" Workshop.	☐ Take December SAT Reasoning Test, SAT Subject Tests, or ACT with Writing.	☐ Mid-December: Colleges notify students of early admissions decisions. ☐ FAFSA financial aid forms available online.

SENIOR YEAR – January

	☐ If necessary, take the January SAT Reasoning Test.	☐ Complete FAFSA online or mail in form.

SENIOR YEAR – January to March

		☐ Submit financial aid documents. ☐ Colleges review applications.

SENIOR YEAR – SPRING – April to May

☐ Receive admission decisions from colleges. ☐ Consider financial aid offers, if necessary. ☐ If waitlisted, let the school know of your continued interest and send additional information that could make a difference. ☐ If you are appealing the denial, send new information that could make a difference. ☐ Thank teachers and counselors for writing letters of recommendation.	☐ Prepare and take May AP Tests.	☐ Colleges notify students of decisions. ☐ Compare financial aid packages. ☐ May 1 common reply date for college with deposit to school you plan to attend. ☐ Check FAFSA acknowledgement, Student Aid Report (SAR) and Pell Grant, if applicable. Complete housing paperwork. ☐ Ask the counselor to mail a final transcript to the school of choice. ☐ Waitlist decisions may be pending.

AFTER GRADUATION

☐ If applicable, apply for Stafford Loan through Lender – this may take up to eight weeks. ☐ Receive orientation schedule from college you plan to attend. ☐ Get resident hall assignment and cost information from the college. ☐ Contact roommate, if assigned one. ☐ Good luck on the next great adventure of your life!		

AN IDEA BEFORE YOU START

*   Keep up with the latest information by subscribing to the College-Path blog RSS feed at:

    http://feeds.feedburner.com/CollegePath

*   You can also follow Dr. Chris on Twitter at:

    https://twitter.com/drchristinehand

*   Or Friend Dr. Chris on the College Path Fan Page on Facebook:

    http://www.facebook.com/pages/College-Pathcom/74842441589

NOTES

II. LEARN THE TERMS FOR THE COLLEGE SEARCH

This section refers to Chapter Two of COLLEGE BOUND.

"It will be helpful to understand the following terminology as you go through the college search and application process. Using the check boxes, test yourself to see how much you know. You'll find more information in the COLLEGE BOUND eBook." – Dr. Chris

☐ **ACT with Writing** – The American College Testing Program test is divided into four parts: English usage, mathematics usage, social science reading, and science reasoning. Score range is 1-36. The national average is 21. The ACT Writing test is a 30-minute essay that measures writing skills.

☐ **Admission Decisions** – The colleges will usually reply in one of five ways: (1) accept, (2) deny, (3) defer (You have not been accepted or denied as an Early Decision or Early Action candidate; therefore, your application will be reviewed in the regular pool of applicants.) (4) waitlist, or (5) admit/deny. (You are admitted but denied financial aid.)

☐ **A.P.** – Advanced Placement courses are considered college-level courses offered in high school for possible college credit. National exams given in May are graded on a scale of 1 (low) to 5 (high).

☐ **B.A.** – Bachelor of Arts is the traditional degree awarded by a liberal arts college or university following the completion of a degree program. You may receive a B.A. in the humanities or the social and natural sciences.

☐ **B.S.** – Bachelor of Science is usually awarded at the completion of a vocationally-oriented program like business, nursing, or education.

☐ **Candidate's Reply Date** – May 1 is the date by which a student must give all accepting colleges a definite "yes" or "no," and send a deposit to the final-choice college.

☐ **College Board** – An association of 2,700 high schools, colleges, universities, and educational systems, the College Board is a major provider of essential educational services and information to students, families, high schools, and colleges. In conjunction with Educational Testing Service (ETS), the College Board sponsors the ATP (Admission Testing Program – PSAT, SAT, SAT Subject Tests, and AP).

☐ **Common Application** – A universal application accepted by over 100 private colleges in lieu of their own applications. An applicant fills out one Common Application and then may mail photocopies to any of the colleges which subscribe to the service.

☐ **College Scholarship Service (CSS)** – A clearinghouse for the Financial Aid Form (FAF). CSS Profile evaluates each FAF, determines the family contribution (what the family can afford to pay), and forwards that analysis to the college Financial Aid Offices and scholarship programs designated by the applicant.

☐ **College Work-Study Program** – CWSP is a federal program, which allows students to pay some of their college expenses by working part time on campus. Eligibility is determined by FAFSA.

☐ **Credit Hour** – The value of a college course according to its level of difficulty. A four-credit course would be more demanding than a three-credit course. Most colleges require a certain number of credit hours for graduation.

☐ **Deferred Admission** – A student applied early or rolling admission to a school, and the college has postponed its decision until a later date in order to receive more data which could include grades, other essays, achievements, or recommendations.

☐ **Deferred Entrance** – A deferred entrance is an admission plan which allows an accepted student to postpone entrance to college for a year while retaining a guarantee of enrollment. During that year the student may work or travel but may not enroll at another college.

☐ **Degree** – There are three basic degrees: Associate's Degree awarded by two-year colleges, Bachelor's Degree awarded by four-year colleges and universities, Master's and other graduate degrees offered by universities.

☐ **Demonstrated Need** – Cost of attending a college or university, minus the family's estimated contribution (as determined either by federal or institutional methodology).

☐ **Demonstrated Interest** – A term used during the admissions process that encourages a student to express a great deal of interest in the institution in order to possibly receive a favorable admission decision.

☐ **Early Action (EA)** – Early Action is an admission plan offered by some highly selective colleges which allows the most qualified students the comfort of a letter of acceptance in December. The student does not have to withdraw other applications and does not have to accept or refuse the EA offer of admission until May 1.

- ☐ **Early Admission** – Early Admissions is an admission plan which allows a student to enter college at the end of the junior year in high school. Admission requirements are usually as stringent as or more so than usual.

- ☐ **Early Decision** – Early Decision is a binding admission plan that requires an early application (typically October or November) and promises a reply by December or January. There are two types of ED plans: (1) Single Choice, in which the student is allowed to apply to only one college and (2) First Choice, in which the student may apply elsewhere but agrees to withdraw other applications if accepted by the ED school. This plan is recommended only if the applicant is absolutely sure of his or her college choice. If accepted, the student is ethically obligated to attend if sufficient financial aid is offered.

- ☐ **Early Notification** – Is an admission plan which promises an early reply to an early application. If accepted, the student is not obligated to attend.

- ☐ **Educational Testing Service (ETS)** – The people responsible for the PSAT, SAT, SAT Subject Tests, and A.P. Exams.

- ☐ **Enrollment Deposit/Matriculation Deposit** – This non-refundable deposit reserves a place in the entering freshman class. Send in by the date specified in the admission materials (usually but not always May 1).

- ☐ **Financial Aid Profile (formerly the FAP)** – The application to the College Scholarship Service is similar in function to the Federal Financial System. The profile is required by some colleges, universities, and scholarship programs to award their own private funds.

- ☐ **Free Application for Federal Student Aid (FAFSA)** – An application form for need-based and federal aid.

- ☐ **GPA** – Grade Point Average is the average of all student grades from freshman year through senior year in high school.

- ☐ **Gapping** – Gapping occurs when an admitted student is awarded a financial aid package that meets less than his or her full demonstrated need.

- ☐ **Liberal Arts** – An introduction to a wide variety of subjects including the social sciences, humanities, fine arts, and natural sciences. The liberal arts do not include such technical majors as engineering, business, allied health, or architecture.

- ☐ **Merit-based Financial Aid** – Financial aid, including scholarships, that is awarded based on a candidate's merit (i.e., academic ability, special talent, competition, audition) excluding athletic aid. It may or may not take into consideration the financial need of the candidate. This aid does not have to be paid back.

- ☐ **Need-based Financial Aid** – Aid offered by colleges and the federal government to bridge the gap between college costs and the family's ability to pay as determined by the profile FFS, FAFSA, and/or the college Financial Aid Office. A typical aid package is divided into three parts: grant (gift money you do not pay back), loan, and work-study (campus job).

- ☐ **Need-blind Admission** – Students are admitted on the basis of academic and personal criteria, regardless of ability to pay. This does not include international students.

- ☐ **Need-conscious (Need-aware, Need-sensitive) Admission** – Financial need might be a factor in the admission decision.

- ☐ **Pell Grants** – Federal grants (gifts, not loans) designed to help students with college costs. Eligibility is determined by the FAFSA.

- ☐ **Preferential/differential Packaging** – The awarding of financial aid packages of differing attractiveness based upon the desirability of the candidates to the admitting institution.

- ☐ **PSAT/NMSQT** – Preliminary Scholastic Assessment Test/National Merit Scholarship Qualifying Test. This test is a shorter version of the SAT given to sophomores and juniors in preparation for the SAT. The PSAT is used to determine eligibility for National Merit and National Achievement Scholarship Programs.

- ☐ **Rolling Admission** – An admission plan in which applications are evaluated very soon after they are completed in the Admission Office. The applicant can receive a decision very quickly but is not obligated to attend.

- ☐ **Regular Decision** – The decision process does not begin until a college accepts applications from prospective students but delays the admission decision until all applications from the entire applicant pool have been received. Decision letters are mailed or emailed to applicants, all at once, traditionally in late March or early April.

☐ **SAT Reasoning Test** – Scholastic Assessment Test is designed to measure a student's verbal and mathematical aptitude as well as writing skills. The score range is 200-800 on each section. The national average is in the 500 range on each part.

☐ **SAT Subject Tests** - Formerly called Achievement Tests, these tests were developed by the College Board to measure a student's knowledge or skills in a particular area and the ability to apply that knowledge. Each test is multiple-choice and takes one hour. Many colleges require the SAT Subject Tests for admission.

☐ **SAT Score Choice** – This option allows the test taker to review his or her SAT and select the scores to be sent to colleges.

☐ **Scholarships** – Some colleges use the term "scholarship" to mean a grant, need-based aid which does not have to be repaid. Other colleges reserve the term "scholarship" for awards given for high academic achievement or special talent, regardless of demonstrated need.

☐ **Student Search** – A College Board service which allows the colleges to receive the names of students who have taken the PSAT or SAT and have indicated their willingness to receive mailings from colleges.

☐ **TOEFL** – Test of English as a Foreign Language is a verbal aptitude test for non-native speakers of English.

☐ **Transcript** – A transcript, an official grade report, shows the final grade you received in each of your courses. It contains personal information: name, address, social security number, date of birth, graduation date, cumulative GPA, total credits earned, courses taken each term, and the signature and seal of the registrar at the high school.

☐ **Waitlist** – The Waitlist is a list of qualified students who may be offered admission by a college at a later date, if space becomes available. Waitlisted students should initially accept another offer of admission and discuss with the college counselor ways to handle the wait list situation.

NOTES

III. THE COLLEGE SEARCH

This section includes the worksheets and checklists referred to in Chapter Three of COLLEGE BOUND.

"Even before beginning the college search, start thinking about what would make a college the right 'fit' for you. Spend time thinking about your strengths, weaknesses, and interests. These checklists, and the many links in the COLLEGE BOUND eBook, will help." – Dr. Chris

HOW DO I FIGURE OUT WHAT TO MAJOR IN?

Some students know what they would like to major in, but others find it a complete mystery. If you are still searching for the area of study that piques your interest, don't panic – many students change their majors at least once in their college careers.

Here are some easy steps to take to narrow down your choice of majors:

- ☐ Complete the O*NET Interest Profiler online by downloading the program - http://www.onenetcenter.org/IP. It is one of the most researched and accepted career exploration tools used by counselors.

- ☐ Complete the Holland Code Assessment. http://www.roguecc.edu/counseling/hollandcodes/test.asp

    HOLLAND CODE three letter code is _____   _____   _____

- ☐ Careers of interest:

    1) _____

    2) _____

    3) _____

- ☐ Conduct a self-assessment and ask yourself these questions: What are my strengths? What are my weaknesses? What are my best subjects and what courses do I like the best in high school? What motivates me?

    _____

    _____

    _____

- ☐ Look through a college course catalogue and register up for classes that pique your interest.

    _____

    _____

- ☐ Complete the Career Interest Game on Rutgers Career Resource site at http://career.missouri.edu./students/majors-careers/skills-interests/career-interest-game. This is a game designed to help you match your interests and skills with similar careers. Holland codes are realistic, investigative, artistic, social, enterprising, and conventional.

    Rank your code: R =_____, I =_____, A =_____, S =_____, E = _____, C = _____

- ☐ Check out major and career profiles through https://bigfuture.collegeboard.org/majors-careers

    List Majors of Interest: 1)_____

    2)_____

    3)_____

- ☐ Use College Navigator website to find the college that has the major related to your career interest-http://nces.ed.gov/collegenavigator/

☐ List colleges of interest:

"Reach" or "Dream" schools:

1) _____

2) _____

3) _____

Possible good fits:

1) _____

2) _____

3) _____

Foundation schools that are likely entries:

1) _____

2) _____

Financial Safety schools with likely admittance:

1)_____

2)_____

☐ Volunteer for an organization for which you think you might like to work.

_____

_____

☐ Observe an adult who has a job that seems interesting to you.

_____

_____

_____

☐ Participate in an internship that will give you a chance to see what the job is all about.

_____

_____

_____

☐ Find a summer or part-time job to "test the waters" in a career area.

_____

_____

_____

☐ Talk to people including classmates, instructors, employers, friends, and family members about college and career choice.

_____

_____

_____

WHOM DO I ASK AND WHERE DO I LOOK FOR COLLEGE INFORMATION?
Check the following resources:

☐ Talk with your guidance counselor and create files on colleges on your list.

☐ Review guide books like *Peterson's*, *Barron's*, or *College Board*.

☐ The Internet is a great resource. Visit college websites, attend college fairs, and meetings at your high school scheduled with admissions representatives. View videos and brochures.

☐ Chat with friends, relatives, neighbors, coaches, and teachers about college.

WHAT POST HIGH SCHOOL PROGRAM MAKES SENSE FOR ME?

☐ **College** - A four-year college grants bachelor's degrees (Bachelor of Arts; Bachelor of Science). Some colleges also award master's degrees.

☐ **University** - A university grants bachelor's and master's degrees, and sometimes includes a professional school such as a law school or medical school. Universities tend to be larger than colleges, focus more on scholarly or scientific research, and might have larger class sizes.

☐ **Community college** - A public two-year college granting associate's degrees and sometimes certificates in particular technical (career-related) subjects. Many students start their postsecondary education at a community college and then transfer to a four-year school, either because a community college tends to be more affordable than a four-year college, or because of the open admissions policy at community colleges.

☐ **Junior college** - A Junior College is similar to a community college, except that a junior college is usually a private school.

☐ **Career school, Technical school, Vocational/Trade school** - These terms are often used interchangeably. These schools may be public or private, offer programs lasting two-years or less-than-two-years. Career schools offer courses that are designed to prepare students for specific careers, from welding to cosmetology to medical imaging and so forth. The difference between technical schools and trade schools is that technical schools teach the science behind the occupation, while trade schools focus on hands-on application of skills needed to do jobs.

"To help decide which type of post high school education would be the best fit for you, take the Self-Assessment on the next page." – Dr. Chris

FINDING THE RIGHT COLLEGE – A SELF-ASSESSMENT

What are your priorities for choosing a college? What would make a college a "perfect fit" for you? You may change your mind over the course of your four years of high school, so you may need to revise your wish list. Check the top ten college characteristics from the list below that are of greatest importance to you.

- ☐ Size of college
- ☐ Location (small town or large city)
- ☐ Distance from home
- ☐ Class size
- ☐ Co-ed or single sex enrollment
- ☐ College's reputation
- ☐ Athletics (Division I, II, III or intramural)
- ☐ Cost (after financial aid and scholarship)
- ☐ Academic requirements for entrance (GPA, coursework, and test scores)
- ☐ Selectivity– easy, moderate, difficult
- ☐ Major you want is offered
- ☐ Resources – library, research opportunities
- ☐ Safety on campus
- ☐ Social activities and student involvement
- ☐ Greek life (fraternities and sororities)
- ☐ Student to faculty ratio
- ☐ Endowment (financial resources)
- ☐ Graduation rate
- ☐ Retention rate
- ☐ Military opportunities – ROTC, academies, enlistment

- ☐ Graduate school placement
- ☐ Job placement
- ☐ Career Services
- ☐ Alumni Satisfaction
- ☐ Friends and family attended (legacy factor) Campus appearance
- ☐ Religious affiliation
- ☐ Type of curriculum – liberal arts, vocational, technical, engineering, etc.
- ☐ Internship opportunities
- ☐ Computer support in the labs and classrooms
- ☐ Student diversity – geographic, economic, racial, ethnic, etc.
- ☐ Honors or Special Programs
- ☐ Friendliness of students and faculty
- ☐ Extracurricular activities
- ☐ Residential or commuter campus
- ☐ Food quality – meal plans; housing
- ☐ Cultural opportunities
- ☐ Types of classroom environment– large or small, discussion or lecture, lab or research
- ☐ Tuition, room and board (meal plan) cost

WHAT COLLEGES LOOK FOR IN STUDENT APPLICANTS

What factors affect the decisions of the college admissions committee? Some carry more weight in the application process than others. These are ranked from most influential to least.

1. Challenging Schedule

2. Academic Performance

3. Standardized Test Scores Consistent with Grades

4. Rank in Class

5. Passionate involvement in Extracurricular Activities

6. Contribution to Community through Volunteer Activities

7. Application Essay – Personal Statement (authenticity, reflective, impact-oriented)

"Tipping" factors that can play a role in admissions:

1. Letters of Recommendation– Counselor/Teacher

2. Socioeconomic Diversity

3. Interview

4. Family Ties and Legacy

5. Internships/Portfolios/Jobs – Out of School Activities

6. Geographic Diversity

7. Academic Diversity

8. Extracurricular Diversity

9. Ethnic/Racial Diversity

COLLEGE VISITS, COLLEGE FAIRS AND COLLEGE VIRTUAL TOURS

Visiting the campus is probably one of the most important steps in actually choosing your college. After all, you may be choosing where you would like to live for the next four years. A visit to the campus will indicate to the admissions representatives that you are interested in their program of study. If you do not have the opportunity to visit, you may have a chance to meet an admissions officer at a college fair in your hometown. Either way, it will be important for you to be prepared.

☐ Do your research about the college ahead of time.

☐ Know your own goals and what questions you would like answered.

☐ Know your PSAT, SAT and/or ACT scores, and GPA.

☐ Be able to talk about your strengths in the academic arena as well as in extracurricular activities.

☐ Avoid the obvious questions – focus more on academic and student life opportunities.

☐ Be yourself, be honest, be prepared, and never underestimate the value of the meeting.

When planning a **visit** to a campus:

☐ Call ahead to schedule the visit, take a tour, and attend an information session.

☐ Arrive on time for your tour.

☐ Dress appropriately – you may be meeting with the admissions representative who may be reviewing your application for admission.

☐ Interact with students, faculty, coaches, and admissions staff.

☐ Pick up a school newspaper.

☐ Attend a class or lecture if possible.

☐ Eat a meal in the dining hall.

☐ View the library and the labs.

☐ Visit a dorm and stay overnight if allowed.

☐ Collect a business card of the admissions person with whom you meet.

After the visit, or **college fair** meeting:

☐ Make notes of your reactions and other important data you may need to consider later in the process.

☐ Ask yourself if the college was a "good fit" for you and your interest.

☐ Send a thank-you note to those with whom you had an appointment.

"In Chapter Three of the COLLEGE BOUND eBook you'll find an extensive list of virtual college tours, college fairs, and career search websites." – Dr. Chris

NOTES

COLLEGE VISIT COMPARISON CHARTS

College Comparison Check List

	College 1	College 2	College 3	College 4	College 5
Undergrad Student Body Size					
Faculty / Student Ratio					
Distance from Home					
Urban / Rural / Suburban					
Numbers of Majors					
Is my major offered here? Yes / No					
Technology					
Special Support Offerings					
Facilities: dorms, dining, laboratories, recreation, etc.					
Research for Undergrads					
Study Abroad Opportunities					
Specific Questions Per College					

Financial Considerations

	College 1	College 2	College 3	College 4	College 5
Is Financial Aid available?					
Are there jobs on campus or Federal Work-Study Programs available?					
Annual In-state Tuition / Out-of-state Tuition & Fees					
Annual Housing Cost					
Annual Meal Plan Cost					
Round-trip Travel Cost					

NOTES

Final Decision Criteria

	College 1	College 2	College 3	College 4	College 5
Can you double major? Will that make you more marketable after graduation?					
Career Placement and Planning: Do you need an advanced degree? Will jobs in your area be sent overseas or available in the U.S.? Does the college hold recruitment fairs?					
Are students accepted to Graduate School and placed satisfactorily?					
Review alumni support and networking opportunities.					
Major Fits / Passion for Study: Internships, research, Co-Op programs, summer work with faculty, and study abroad opportunities.					
Level of credentials of professors teaching your major.					
Environment fits me Best: Accessibility to home, city, suburb or rural, college-town feel.					
Size of Student Population – Is it what I'm looking for?					
Financial Check: School matches my budget/offers financial aid, and scholarship possibilities all four years.					
Level of satisfaction with living space.					
Extracurricular activities fit needs.					

Rate Programs by FSP Index (Faculty Scholarly Productivity) The Chronicle of Higher Education http://chronicle.com/stats/productivity/ and research productivity, grants, publications and academic awards.
  - Talk with others, but make your own decision
  - Go with your "gut feeling" in the end
  - Don't stress – students do change their minds and transfer					

IV. THE COLLEGE APPLICATION PROCESS

This section includes the worksheets and checklists referred to in Chapter Four of COLLEGE BOUND.

"Chapter Four of COLLEGE BOUND covers all aspects of the college application process from completing forms, discussing standardized test options, building a substantial resume of activities, to offering ways for students to improve their chances of admission, and much more. The forms below will help you through the process." – Dr. Chris

ADMISSION PROCEDURES: WHICH ADMISSION OPTION IS RIGHT FOR YOU?

Each individual is unique; therefore, the number of schools you choose to apply to is up to you. Most students pare their foundation list of colleges to a final five to seven schools. Be sure to include a long shot — a **stretch school** — a reach — a college where your chances of gaining admission are less than 50% based upon your academic profile when compared to students the admission office admitted in the previous year.

1) _____

2) _____

3) _____

A reasonable reach — 50/50 or better – colleges are likely to admit within the student's range of grade point average, standardized test scores, and course curriculum. Other factors that could enhance admission status could include activities, an interview, special talents, recommendations, essays, etc.

1) _____

2) _____

3) _____

Likely schools — "sure shots" are colleges where a student is confident of admission. However, be sure it is a school where your academic and personal needs will be met if you enroll.

1) _____

2) _____

3) _____

Financial safety schools — these are colleges where a student is confident that he or she may be admitted and can afford to pay. However, be sure it is a school where your academic and personal needs will be met should you enroll.

1) _____

2) _____

The best way to create this list is to research colleges by visiting the campus, taking tours, and speaking with admissions representatives. Review what is required to apply to the colleges including grade point average, high school course requirements, standardized test scores, resume of activities, essays, and recommendations.

APPLICATION JARGON AND DEADLINES

The **application deadline** is the date by which all completed applications are due to the college. In some cases the date will be a postmark date; in others, it will be a date by which all material must be received. It will be helpful to read the section called, "How to Apply" on each college's website.

Early Action – Early Action is an admission plan offered by some highly selective colleges which allows the most qualified students the comfort of a letter of acceptance in December. The student does not have to withdraw other applications and does not have to accept or refuse the EA offer of admission until May 1.

Early Decision – Early Decision is a binding admission plan that requires an early application (typically October or November) and promises a reply by December or January. There are two types of ED plans: (1) Single Choice, in which the student is allowed to apply to only one college and (2) First Choice, in which the student may apply elsewhere but agrees to withdraw other applications if accepted by the ED school. This plan is recommended only if the applicant is absolutely sure of his or her college choice. If accepted, the student is ethically obligated to attend if sufficient financial aid is offered.

Rolling Admission – An admission plan in which applications are evaluated very soon after they are completed in the Admission Office. The applicant can receive a decision very quickly but is not obligated to attend.

Regular Decision – is the process whereby a college accepts applications from prospective students and delays the admission decision until all applications from the entire applicant pool have been received. Decision letters are mailed or emailed to all applicants, at once, traditionally in late March or early April.

Waitlist – The Waitlist is a group of qualified students who may be offered admission by a college at a later date, if space becomes available.

Candidate's Reply Date – May 1 is the date by which a student must give all accepting colleges a definite "yes" or "no," and send a deposit to the final-choice college.

THE ULTIMATE COLLEGE APPLICATION CHECKLIST

CHECKLIST OF THINGS TO DO	College 1	College 2	College 3	College 4
Campus Visit.				
Campus Interview (if required).				
Resumes of activities, academics, and achievements to a counselor and a teacher for letter of recommendation.				
Teacher Recommendation 1 - Date requested - Stamped envelopes addressed to admissions office or email address if recommendations sent electronically.				
Teacher Recommendation 2- Date requested- Stamped envelopes addressed to admissions office or email address if recommendations sent electronically.				
Letters of Recommendation – Peer review or optional writer of letter of recommendation as required by college.				
Counselor recommendation letter and/ or Secondary School Report Form to counselor if not sent electronically. Send thank-you note.				
Follow-up and thank-you notes written.				
Test scores requested and sent from College Board (ETS) or ACT to colleges.				
Transcripts sent from high school(s) to colleges.				
If student-athlete, NCAA Eligibility Center form submitted and transcript sent				
Auditions scheduled if theater, dance, or music performance student.				
Portfolio completed for students applying to fine arts program.				
Military application completed including physical, letters of nomination, recommendations, and application.				
Application completed.				

Essay(s) completed.				
Financial aid forms from college enclosed.				
FAFSA and/or CSS Profile completed by deadlines.				
Application fee processed if online, enclosed if paper application.				
Postage affixed/copies made/return address on envelopes sent to the college.				
Copies made of all forms and documentation enclosed in application packet if applying online.				
Letters of acceptance/denial/waitlist received by April 1.				
Colleges notified of intent by May 1.				
Tuition deposit sent to one college of choice by May 1.				
Housing and other forms submitted to chosen college by May 1.				
Ask high school counselor to send final transcript to one college.				
Orientation and course registration at college scheduled.				

NOTES

COMPLETING THE COLLEGE APPLICATION

Before you begin completing your college applications, it will help you to review the basic tips provided here to prevent application overload.

Start early! Give yourself plenty of time to produce a stellar final product. You want a winning application, not one that looks harried and rushed.

Have the following pieces of information on hand before you start to fill out your application. It's not a bad idea to save this information on a card or in a computer file.

- ☐ Your social security number
  - Personal information including address, phone, and other demographic information
- ☐ Family information
  - Father's Name, address, date of birth, and occupation
  - Mother's name, address, date of birth, and occupation
  - Father's college, degree, and date of graduation
  - Mother's college, degree, and date of graduation
  - Sibling's name(s), age(s), and college(s) attended
- ☐ Your transcript
  - Courses taken
  - Grade Point Average; Class Rank
  - Test Scores (SAT and ACT)
  - Extracurricular Activities in order of importance
  - Honors and Awards
- ☐ School information
  - SAT and ACT code
  - Counselor's phone and fax number and school address
  - Teacher(s) for recommendation section (if applicable)
- ☐ Student work history
  - Name of employer and dates employed

THE COMMON APPLICATION

View a sample student application, counselor/secondary report form, and teacher recommendation from http://www.commonapp.org. Additional information may be needed if you plan to attend a military academy, plan to play sports, or focus on the arts.

To download a form, just click on a link on the next page. You will need Adobe Acrobat Reader - http://get.adobe.com/reader/ - to open all files below. With the exception of the Application (student form), you can type data into any of the forms below before printing, though you cannot save that data into a PDF unless you purchased Adobe Acrobat Professional.

Complete First-Year Application Packet –

https://www.commonapp.org/

- Instructions
- Application (student form
- Deadlines and Requirements GRID
- Decision Plan Rules
- Arts Supplement
- Athletic Supplement
- Early Decision (ED) Agreement
- Teacher Evaluation
- School Report
- Optional Report
- Mid-year Report
- Final Report
- International School Supplement to the School Report
- Home School Supplement to the School Report
- College-specific Supplements

If considering a transfer from another college, complete Transfer Application Packet - https://www.commonapp.org/

- Transfer Application
- Instructor Evaluation
- College Official's Form
- Midterm Report
- Secondary School Final Report
- College-specific Supplements

To download completed online application you will need Adobe Acrobat Reader - http://get.adobe.com/reader/.

http://www.adobe.com/products/acrobat/readstep2.html

"For up-to-date tips and information, follow my blog at www.College-Path.com.

Follow me on Twitter ID: https://twitter.com/drchristinehand.

"Like" the College Path Fan Page on Facebook at http://www.facebook.com/pages/College-Pathcom/74842441589.

"Subscribe to our RSS Feed: http://feeds.feedburner.com/CollegePath." – Dr. Chris

 **COUNSELOR GUIDE TO THE APPLICATION**

This guide displays the sections and pages within The Common Application. It is designed to familiarize students with the information they will be asked to report and is not intended to be a comprehensive collection of all questions within the application.

PROFILE	**Contacts** *Email address, phone number, mailing address* **Demographics** *Religion, military service, race/ethnicity (all optional)* **Geography** *Birthplace, countries lived in, language proficiency, citizenship*
FAMILY	**Household** *Parent marital status, parent(s) with whom you reside* **Parent and/or Guardian** *Name, birthplace, occupation, education, stepparent information* **Siblings** *Age, grade, education*
EDUCATION	**School** *Current school, dates attended; counselor name, phone, and email* **History** *Previous schools, dates attended, past/pending education interruptions (e.g. time off, early graduation, gap year, etc.), college courses, college assistance programs* **Academic Information** *GPA, class rank, current year courses, honors and awards*
TESTING	**College Entrance** *ACT and SAT* **English For Non-Native Speakers** *TOEFL, IELTS, PTE Academic* **Academic Subjects** *AP, IB, SAT Subject Tests, A-Levels* **Other** *Optional reporting for other relevant 9-12 testing*
ACTIVITIES	**Principal Activities/Work** *Years of participation, hours per week, weeks per year, position/leadership held (50 characters), brief description (150 characters). 10 activities maximum.*

ESSAY	**Select One, 650 Words Maximum** • Some students have a background or story that is so central to their identity that they believe their application would be incomplete without it. If this sounds like you, then please share your story. • Recount an incident or time when you experienced failure. How did it affect you, and what lessons did you learn? • Reflect on a time when you challenged a belief or idea. What prompted you to act? Would you make the same decision again? • Describe a place or environment where you are perfectly content. What do you do or experience there, and why is it meaningful to you? • Discuss an accomplishment or event, formal or informal, that marked your transition from childhood to adulthood within your culture, community, or family.
EXPLANATIONS	**Required Responses** Explanations regarding school discipline[1], criminal history[2], education interruption, veteran discharge status
ADDITIONAL INFO	**Optional Responses** Relevant circumstances or qualifications not reflected elsewhere in the application
COLLEGE PAGE 1	**General** Entry term, degree status, housing preference, test-optional preference, scholarship and financial aid preference **Academics** Academic interest, program(s) applying to **Contacts** Interactions with the institution (campus visit, off-campus interview, etc.) **Family** Family members who have attended or been employed by the institution **Evaluations** Names of classroom teachers, coaches, other recommenders **Residence** Required by some public institutions to determine in-state status **Signature** Acknowledgments and affirmations (Not all member colleges will ask all questions.)
COLLEGE PAGE 2	**Writing Supplement** Additional short answer or essay responses if requested by institution

1. Have you ever been found responsible for a disciplinary violation at any educational institution you have attended from the 9th grade (or the international equivalent) forward, whether related to academic misconduct or behavioral misconduct, that resulted in a disciplinary action? These actions could include, but are not limited to: probation, suspension, removal, dismissal, or expulsion from the institution.

2. Have you ever been adjudicated guilty or convicted of a misdemeanor, felony, or other crime? Note that you are not required to answer "yes" to this question, or provide an explanation, if the criminal adjudication or conviction has been expunged, sealed, annulled, pardoned, destroyed, erased, impounded, or otherwise ordered by a court to be kept confidential.

SCHOOL REPORT

CONTACTS

Official Name / Title	Name and contact info for official completing form
Email / Phone	
Website / Profile	
School / CEEB	
Address	

Identifying information prints from the student's account. FERPA will show as Waived or Not Waived depending on student's online selection.

SCHOOL PROFILE   School Profile data should be completed to the extent possible.

College Bound	_____% Four-Year _____% Two-Year
Ethnicity	_____% Asian _____% Black _____% Latino _____% White _____% Native
First Gen	_____% First-Generation
International	_____% US Citizens _____% Non-US Citizens
Socioeconomic	_____% Receive Free or Reduced Lunch
Financial Aid	_____% Receive Financial Aid (Independent Schools)
Setting	☐ Rural ☐ Suburban ☐ Urban
Curriculum	Total Offered/Yearly Limit AP _____ / _____ Honors _____ / _____ IB _____ / _____
	IB Diploma Candidate? ☐ Yes ☐ No Block Schedule ☐ Yes ☐ No
Attached Grades	☐ 11: Final ☐ 12: 1st Quarter ☐ 12: 2nd Quarter/1st Semester
	☐ 12: 1st Trimester ☐ 12: 2nd Trimester ☐ 12: 3rd Quarter ☐ 12: Final
Graduation	_____ (m/d/y)

"Attached Grades" refers to the most recent grades reflected on the accompanying transcript.

TO BE COMPLETED BY INTERNATIONAL SCHOOLS THAT DO NOT USE AN AP CURRICULUM

Language of Instruction _____

Promotion based on a state or national exam?	☐ Yes	☐ No
If so, has student taken leaving exams?	☐ Yes	☐ No

These questions replace the International School Supplement.

Grading/Marking Scale	A _____	B _____	C _____	D _____	F _____
	Excellent	*Very Good*	*Average*	*Poor*	*Failing*

If applicable, please attach an official copy of this student's lower secondary examination results. If the student has already taken senior secondary leaving exams, please include an official copy of the results. If this applicant's senior secondary leaving exam results are not yet available, please attach predicted results.

HOME SCHOOL SUPERVISORS SHOULD ATTACH AND EXPLAIN:

• Name of homeschooler's association, if applicable: _These questions replace the Home School Supplement._
• Any information about the applicant's home school experience and environment that you believe would be helpful to the reader (e.g. educational philosophy, motivation for home schooling, instruction setting, etc.).
• Grading scale or other methods of evaluation.
• Any distance learning, traditional secondary school, or higher education coursework not included on the transcript. List the course title and content, sponsoring institution, instruction setting and schedule, and frequency of interactions with instructors and fellow students (once per day, week, etc.).
• Standardized testing beyond what is collected in the Common Application.

ACADEMICS

Class Rank _____ Class Size _____ Covering a period from (m/y) _____ to _____

The rank is ☐weighted ☐unweighted. How many additional students share this rank? _____

Cumulative GPA: _____ on a _____ scale, covering a period from (m/y) _____ to _____

This GPA is ☐weighted ☐unweighted. The school's passing mark is: _____

Highest GPA in class _____

In comparison with other college preparatory students at your school, the applicant's course selection is:
☐Most demanding ☐Very demanding ☐Demanding ☐Average ☐Below average

RATINGS

No Basis		Below Average	Average	Good (above average)	Very Good (Well above average)	Excellent (top 10%)	Outstanding (top 5%)	Top few (top 1%)
	Academic achievement							
	Extracurricular Accomplishments							
	Personal qualities and character							
	OVERALL							

SR *FirstName LastName RD FY Fall 2014 01/01/95 CEEB: 000000 CAID: **0000000***

EVALUATION

How long have you known this student, and in what context? _____
_____

What are the first words that come to your mind to describe this student? _____
_____

COMMENTS

Please provide comments that will help us differentiate this student from others. Feel free to attach an additional sheet or another reference you have prepared for this student. Alternatively, you may attach a reference written by another school official who can better describe the student.

Has the applicant ever been found responsible for a disciplinary violation at your school from the 9th grade (or the international equivalent) forward, whether related to academic misconduct or behavioral misconduct, that resulted in a disciplinary action? These actions could include, but are not limited to: probation, suspension, removal, dismissal, or expulsion from your institution.

☐Yes ☐No ☐School policy prevents me from responding

To your knowledge, has the applicant ever been adjudicated guilty or convicted of a misdemeanor, felony, or other crime?

☐Yes ☐No ☐School policy prevents me from responding.

Note that you are not required to answer "yes" to this question, or provide an explanation, if the criminal adjudication or conviction has been expunged, sealed, annulled, pardoned, destroyed, erased, impounded, or otherwise ordered to be kept confidential by a court.

If you answered "yes" to either or both questions, please attach a separate sheet of paper or use your written recommendation to give the approximate date of each incident and explain the circumstances.

Applicants are expected to immediately notify the institutions to which they are applying should there be any changes to the information requested in this application, including disciplinary history.

☐ Check here if you would prefer to discuss this applicant over the phone with each admission office.

I recommend this student: ☐No basis ☐With reservation ☐Fairly strongly ☐Strongly ☐Enthusiastically

Signature _____

Please mail this form and accompanying documents directly to the each college/university admission office. Do not mail this form to The Common Application offices.

SR *FirstName LastName RD FY Fall 2014 01/01/95 CEEB: 000000 CAID: **0000000***

TEACHER EVALUATION

CONTACTS

Official Name / Title   Name and contact info for official completing form

Email / Phone

School / CEEB

Address

> Identifying information prints from the student's account. FERPA will show as Waived or Not Waived depending on student's online selection.

EVALUATION

In what subject did you teach this student? _____

How long have you known the student, and in what context? _____

What are the first words that come to mind to describe this student? _____

In which grade level(s) was the student enrolled when you taught him/her?   9☐   10☐   11☐   12☐

Other _____

List the courses in which you have taught this student, including the level of course difficulty (AP, IB, accelerated, honors, elective; 100-level, 200-level; etc.)

_____

_____

_____

COMMENTS

Please attach additional comments that address what you think is important about this student, including a description of academic and personal characteristics, as demonstrated in your classroom. We welcome information that will help us to differentiate this student from others. (Feel free to attach another reference you may have already prepared on behalf of this student.)

TE *FirstName LastName RD FY Fall 2014 01/01/95*
CEEB: 000000 CAID: ***0000000***

RATINGS

No Basis		Below Average	Average	Good (above average)	Very Good (Well above average)	Excellent (top 10%)	Outstanding (top 5%)	Top few (top 1%)
	Academic Achievement							
	Intellectual Promise							
	Writing							
	Creativity							
	Class Discussion							
	Faculty Respect							
	Work Habits							
	Maturity							
	Motivation							
	Leadership							
	Integrity							
	Resilience							
	Collaborative							
	Self-confidence							
	Initiative							
	OVERALL							

Signature _____

Please mail this form and accompanying documents directly to the each college/university admission office. Do not mail this form to The Common Application offices.

TE *FirstName LastName RD FY Fall 2014 01/01/95*
*CEEB: 000000 CAID: **0000000***

COLLEGE APPLICATION INFORMATION WEBSITES

In Chapter Four of the **COLLEGE BOUND** book you can access important websites for the application process.

There are several types of standardized tests used for college admissions. Each one has a purpose, and these tests give the college admissions representatives an idea of a student's college readiness. The admissions committee will often look at these scores in conjunction with the grade point average and rigor of courses taken by the student. The tests are the SAT, SAT Subject Test, ACT with Writing, TOEFL, and AP (Advanced Placement Tests).

SAT Reasoning Test is a standardize test which measures a student's verbal and mathematical aptitude as well as writing skills. Score range is 600-2400.

SAT Subject Tests were developed by the College Board to measure the student's knowledge or skills in a certain area such as math, history, physical science, literature, and foreign language. These tests can be taken at any point in the student's junior or senior year as long as he or she has completed the related course work in that subject area.

ACT with Writing is also taken nationally like the SAT. It focuses on English usage, mathematics usage, social science reading, and science reading. An optional writing section is recommended by most colleges. Score range is 1-36 on the ACT.

TOEFL evaluates non-native English speakers' ability to read, write, speak, and listen to English similar to the way it is used at the university level. The sections covered include Reading, Listening, Speaking, and Writing.

AP or advanced placement tests are considered college-level course given in high school for possible college credit. Score range from 1-5. Students should check with the colleges they are applying to see if they accept AP credits. Some colleges will offer credit for a score of 3, though most require a 4 or 5.

Students are reminded to submit their scores directly to the colleges they are applying to.

Quick Tips for Prepping for the Test

Start soon enough to make a difference. Students should give themselves an adequate amount of time to prepare for the various subject areas. Sufficient preparation will leave you feeling less rushed and reduce anxiety. Various test preparation tools are available such as study guides, flashcards, Internet programs and CDs produced by the testing companies. Be sure to get enough sleep the night before the test. The student should read, read, read to build reading comprehension skills.

On Testing Day

- ☐ Eat well and bring a snack for the break
- ☐ Bring the right supplies - photo ID, #2 pencils
- ☐ Get to the test center site early
- ☐ Wear comfortable clothes
- ☐ Know the procedures
- ☐ Review the whole test section before you start
- ☐ Answer easy questions first
- ☐ In the ACT, answer every question because no deductions are taken for incorrect answers
- ☐ Identify key words
- ☐ Rephrase difficult questions
- ☐ Eliminate answers on multiple choice sections
- ☐ Jot down your thoughts
- ☐ Write neatly
- ☐ Use all of the time given

NOTES

ACT VS. SAT

Colleges will accept either the ACT or the SAT. Some colleges do not require either, but these institutions will place more emphasis on the grade point average and the rigor of the students' coursework; to get this list, go to http://www.Fairtest.org.

	ACT	SAT
Length of Test	3 hours, 25 minutes (including optional 30-minutes Writing section)	3 hours, 45 minutes
Sections	4 Sections (plus optional Writing section): English, Math , Reading, Science, Writing	10 Sections: 3 Critical Reading, 3 Math, Writing (including Essay) and 1 Experimental section (not scored)
Subjects	English, Math, Reading, Science and Writing (optional)	Critical Reading, Math and Writing
Reading	4 passages, 10 questions per passage	Reading passages with questions pertaining to comprehension, and sentence completion
Science	Science (analysis, knowledge, problem solving)	Not applicable
Math	Arithmetic, Algebra, Geometry, and Trigonometry	Arithmetic, Algebra, Geometry, and Trigonometry
Essay	Optional (final section)	Required
Score Composition	1/4 English, 1/4 Math, 1/4 Reading, 1/4 Science	1/3 Math, 1/3 Reading,1/3 Writing
Scoring	Based on Composite Score of 1-36 points for each section, 0-12 for Optional Essay	Score of 600-2400 based on total of 3 scores (Reading, Math and Writing) Essay score range from 0-12
Penalties	No penalties for incorrect answers	1/4 point deducted for wrong answers
Sending Scores to Colleges	All scores from the selected test date(s) will be sent. Students can choose which test date to send	Students decide which scores are sent (may use Score Choice option or not)
Websites for More Information	www.act.org	www.collegeboard.com

SAT/ACT CONCORDANCE CHART

The ACT and SAT are different tests that measure similar but distinct constructs. The ACT measures achievement related to high school curricula, while the SAT measures general verbal and quantitative reasoning.

ACT and the College Board have completed a concordance study that is designed to examine the relationship between two scores on the ACT and SAT. These concordance tables do not equate scores; rather, they provide a tool for finding comparable scores.

SAT/ACT Concordance Chart

ACT *If you scored...*	CURRENT SAT *or...*	NEW SAT *It's about the same as...*
36	1600	2400
35	1560-1590	2340
34	1510-1550	2260
33	1460-1500	2190
32	1410-1450	2130
31	1360-1400	2040
30	1320-1350	1980
29	1280-1310	1920
28	1240-1270	1860
27	1210-1230	1820
26	1170-1200	1760
25	1130-1160	1700
24	1090-1120	1650
23	1060-1080	1590
22	1020-1050	1530
21	980-1010	1500
20	940-970	1410
19	900-930	1350
18	860-890	1290
17	810-850	1210
16	760-800	1140
15	710-750	1060
14	660-700	1000
13	590-650	900
12	520-580	780
11	500-510	750

Download: ACT *(PDF; 2 pages, 30KB)*
ACT/College Board Joint Statement and Tables *(PDF; 4 pages, 69KB)* See also, Estimated Relationship between ACT Composite Score and SAT CR+M+W Score. © ACT.org

SAT SCORE CHOICE

Score Choice allows the students to forward the scores they choose to the colleges or universities they are applying to. So, what does a student need to know about this policy?

Here are some items to think about:

- ☐ SAT Reasoning and Subject test scores can be submitted by test date. If a student does not choose Score Choice, all scores will be sent to the college.

- ☐ Score Choice is optional.

- ☐ Students should follow the score-reporting requirements of their colleges.

- ☐ Colleges will only receive the scores that the student sends to them.

- ☐ Individual sections of a specific test date cannot be selected—only the entire test of the particular SAT will be sent.

- ☐ It does not cost more to send one or multiple copies or all SAT test scores to a college.

- ☐ Scores can be sent by paper, CD, or Electronic Score Reports. If the student requests a second report to a college, the report will only include the unique set of scores chosen by the student, which may or may not include previous test scores.

- ☐ For more information, check with the http://www.CollegeBoard.com.

STANDARDIZED TEST PREPARATION AND INFORMATION WEBSITES
"In the COLLEGE BOUND book you will find a number of live links to FREE test preparation websites!" – Dr. Chris

THE IMPORTANCE OF AN ACTIVITIES RESUME

Involvement in extracurricular activities can make you stand out in the college application process. Are you a leader? Have you achieved a noteworthy level of achievement? How does the activity make you distinctly different from others with similar interests?

This same resume will also be helpful for teachers and counselors whom you may ask to write your letter of recommendation. So gather the following information: name, address, professional email address, cell phone/home phone number, objective or summary, education, extracurricular activities, volunteer service, awards and certificates, skills/academic achievement, music /artistic achievements, references, and other information.

"Sample resumes can be found in the COLLEGE BOUND book in Chapter Four." – Dr. Chris

Name _____

Mailing Address_____

Email Address _____ Cell Phone Number _____

Profile example:

High School senior skilled in athletics and working with children in sports-related activities; dependable and mature; seeking admission to a college where I can study Sports Medicine.

Education

HS Diploma: Graduation Date _____ from _____ High School, Town, State, Zip Code

GPA: _____ **SAT:** Critical Reading _____ Math _____ Writing _____ **ACT:** Composite _____ **ACT Writing** _____

AP Courses Completed

_____

_____

_____

Honors and Awards (title and year)

_____

_____

_____

Extracurricular Activities (name of activity, position, dates of participation)

_____

_____

_____

Community Service (name of activity, title, and dates of participation)

_____

_____

Employment (title, place, town, date of the job, specify job held and duties performed)

_____

_____

Additional Training (coursework, date completed)

_____

_____

_____

_____

_____

HOW TO REQUEST A LETTER OF RECOMMENDATION

Colleges may require a letter of recommendation, or they may not. You will need to review what each school requires as part of the application. There are several people who may need to write on your behalf; your counselor and/or a teacher. Sometimes colleges will specify what they are looking for more specifically, like a letter from a teacher who taught you your junior year or the one who taught you in a core course like English, math, science, history or foreign language. Review the following tips to help you get an effective letter of recommendation:

- ☐ The letter should be from someone who knows you well. He or she will need to be able to produce a well-written piece that will help the admissions office learn something new about you.

- ☐ Set a time to speak with the individual you would like to write your letter. Share a resume of activities and academic achievements that will help him or her develop an initial letter. Anecdotes and illustrations will help create an image of what your strengths and interests.

- ☐ Be sure to give the deadline when the letter is due to the college as well as a stamped, addressed envelope to the admissions office, unless it is to be submitted electronically.

- ☐ Give the person at least four weeks in advance of the deadline. Ask in person – not by email.

- ☐ Additional recommendations may be appropriate, but consult with your college counselor for sure. One additional recommendation from an employer or supervisor, a mentor, or a leader in the community, that provides additional information that may not be found in the teacher or counselor evaluation is acceptable, but more than one is generally discouraged.

- ☐ Send a thank-you note in a few weeks to show your appreciation for submitting this information on your behalf.

- ☐ Once you hear of your acceptances, it would be nice to let the person know the outcome since he or she had a hand in the process with you.

"Complete the form on the next page, making as many copies as you need, and give them to your college recommenders. Many recommendations can be submitted electronically, but for those that cannot, include a stamped envelope addressed to 'Undergraduate Admissions Office' and give them to the writer of your recommendation." – Dr. Chris

COLLEGE RECOMMENDATION FORM

Complete this form, making as many copies as you need, and give them to those individuals writing your letter of recommendation. Include a stamped envelope addressed to the Undergraduate Admissions Office.

Name:_____ _____ _____
               Last   First   Middle

I.D.#_____ E-mail _____Cell phone_____

I. FAMILY

Check the college attended and highest degree earned by each:

Mother	_____	Associate's Bachelor's Master's Doctorate
Father	_____	Associate's Bachelor's Master's Doctorate
Brother(s)	_____	Associate's Bachelor's Master's Doctorate
	_____	Associate's Bachelor's Master's Doctorate
Sister(s)	_____	Associate's Bachelor's Master's Doctorate
	_____	Associate's Bachelor's Master's Doctorate

II. ACTIVITIES (check years participated)

Activity	9	10	11	12	Level of involvement

III. COMMUNITY/NON-HIGH SCHOOL - ACTIVITIES

Religious organizations, summer programs, volunteer (check years participated), work, etc.

9	10	11	12	Level of involvement

IV. WORK EXPERIENCE

Employer/ Position / Title/ Hours/ Week Length of Employment

_____

_____

_____

_____

V. COLLEGE/CAREER GOALS AND ACADEMIC INTEREST

List all colleges to which you are applying: Deadline Date for Recommendation

_____

_____

What major/area of study are you considering for college? "Undecided" is ok.

_____

_____

What career(s) are you considering pursuing?

_____

_____

Do you feel that your transcript accurately reflects your academic ability? Yes / No

If no, explain what factors/circumstances have interfered with your academic performance?

_____

_____

_____

What do you think are your academic strengths? Give examples.

_____

_____

_____

List 3 academic faculty members (preferably junior year) who could give you a positive appraisal and list reasons.

_____

_____

_____

VI. PERSONAL

Who are your personal heroes, men and women you admire, and why?

_____

_____

_____

_____

_____

What special interests or hobbies do you pursue outside of school?

_____

_____

_____

What personal experience, summer experience, school/work experience, or travel has been of significant importance to you, and why?

_____

_____

_____

Is there any information you would like for me to emphasize in my recommendation to help the colleges make a more accurate appraisal of your application? Let me know what else you would like me to include or emphasize.

_____

_____

_____

_____

_____

_____

_____

_____

_____

_____

_____

_____

_____

_____

_____

_____

_____

_____

_____

_____

_____

_____

_____

Self-Evaluation

Read the statements and rate yourself using the scale below.

RATINGS	Below Average	Average	Good	Excellent	Outstanding
Ability to organize/use time					
Self-confidence					
Desire to learn new information					
Willingness to take risks					
Ability to get along with others					
Willingness to work hard					
Imagination/Creativity					
Ability to express self					
Sense of humor					
Concern for others					
Emotional maturity					
Reaction to setbacks					
Understanding new concepts					
Self-discipline					
Growth potential					
Leadership					
Energy					
Motivation					
Warmth of personality					
Personal initiative					
Respect accorded to faculty					

Circle five descriptive words and provide an example of the way each word applies to you.

Example: I am very creative. I work on the Win-Win magazines and I had some of my photos featured in the publication...

accountable	diplomatic	knowledgeable	realistic	active
discerning	reflective	adaptable	disciplined	leads
reliable	adept	discrete	resourceful	aggressive
economical	loyal	respected	alert	responsible
ambitious	efficient	mature	responsive	analytical
empathetic	methodical	articulate	energetic	mobile
self-directed	assertive	enterprising	motivated	self-reliant
attentive	enthusiastic	sense-of-humor	experienced	objective
sensitive	broad-minded	expert	observant	serious
capable	expressive	open-minded	clever	sincere
charismatic	extroverted	optimistic	skilled	organized
sophisticated	collaborative	fair	outgoing	spontaneous
committed	forceful	communicative	patient	stimulating
competent	goal-oriented	perceptive	strong	concise
persevering	sympathetic	confident	helpful	personable
systematic	conscientious	honest	persuasive	consistent
humorous	pleasant	tactful	constructive	poised
talented	conversant	imaginative	positive	team-oriented
cooperative	implements	practical	tenacious	creative
improvises	precise	tolerant	critical	independent
solves problem	curious	industrious	productive	understanding
innovative	professional	decisive	instinctive	proficient
versatile	dependable	intelligent	proven	vigorous
determined	intuitive	warm	well-read	well-rounded

College List and Student Questionnaire for Counselor Recommendation

Name

_____

Phone

_____

Address

_____

_____

_____

Directions

Fill out the following questions as completely as possible. This information is extremely important and will be used by your counselor in composing your letter of recommendation. Give your counselor a minimum of 4 week notice. Include stamped envelope to the office of undergraduate admissions with a return address of your school.

I give my counselor permission to send a letter of recommendation, transcript, and school profile to my colleges. _____initials

College Information

Please list the colleges you will be applying to this year. *__Make sure you include a likely to be admitted and financial safety school.__*

Name of College   *EA/ED/REGD/ROLLING   Deadline Date Letter and/or Forms Requested

* Early Action/Early Decision/ Regular Decision/ Rolling Admission

1.	
2.	
3.	
4.	
5.	
6.	
7.	
8.	
Likely to be admitted and "Financial Safety" school	
1.	
2.	

Recommendations

Write the names of the teacher(s) you will ask to write your letter(s) of recommendation:

1. _____

2. _____

Personal Information

Apart from your resume, your counselor would like to know more about you in order to distinguish you as a student. Although you do not need to answer every question, please complete as many of the statements below as thoroughly as possible. The more **depth** you provide, the more your counselor has to work with in presenting your contributions, accomplishments, and special attributes.

1. Please write your senior quote below or record a special quote or saying which you feel is significant. Indicate why you selected this quote and what important meaning it has for you.

2. The activity I have contributed the most to and/or the activity that has meant the most to me is...

3. My greatest moment at my school was when...

4. If they could see into my future, they would see me at college actively involved in...

5. My dreams for the future include a job where I could...

6. Something you would be surprised to know about me is...

7. I would like my counselor to make special mention of this aspect about me or my life circumstances in my letter of recommendation OR what qualities would you like mentioned that really distinguish you as a college applicant?

8. I would also like to mention... (Have you had to work? Why? What summer programs/study have you participated in? Do you speak more than one language?)

Character/Anecdotal Statement

Optional

Name of Student   _____

Name of Writer   _____

Relationship to Student _____

Directions to the Student: Have this form filled out by someone who knows you well. This could be a parent, grandparent, older brother or sister, or community member. This statement will **not** be considered confidential so do read and approve it before giving it to your counselor.

Directions to the Writer: The job of the counselor is to write a comprehensive letter distinguishing this student's academic accomplishments and unique character qualities.

Please choose one of the following ideas and write a short statement on behalf of this person. This information will be considered by the student's counselor in writing a letter of recommendation. This information will **not** be considered confidential.

- ☐   Is there a story or event which would exemplify the positive character traits of this person? Describe.

- ☐   What do you most admire about this student? Are there any incidents that show these qualities?

- ☐   What would you want this counselor to include in a letter of recommendation for this person?

Please write below or type on a separate sheet.

     My College Bound Plan 2013 / 2014 Edition – Copyright 2013 College Path LLC – All Rights Reserved.

THE COLLEGE ESSAY

- ☐ Start early.

- ☐ Write about something with which you're familiar.

- ☐ Be yourself.

- ☐ Be original.

- ☐ Write an essay that shows how you're unique.

- ☐ Include any experiences or jobs that might set you apart from other applicants.

- ☐ Be authentic; be real.

- ☐ Use a relaxed, comfortable tone of voice but avoid being too familiar, sarcastic, or comical.

- ☐ Check to make sure your essay answers the questions asked. Avoid wandering from your subject matter.

- ☐ Review, review, review. Proofread your essay for spelling, punctuation, and grammar.

- ☐ Mail your application early to avoid any postal mishap or Internet complications.

"Check out websites that can be helpful in the Essay Writing section of Chapter Four in the COLLEGE BOUND book."

TIPS FOR THE COLLEGE INTERVIEW AND SAMPLE QUESTIONS

Admission Procedures	Admissions Testing	Academic Programs	Technology Use	Student Life

Not all schools require or offer an interview. However, if you are offered an interview, use this one-on-one time to evaluate the college in detail and to promote yourself to the admissions representative. Do your research on the basic information and ask more specific questions about the topics shown above.

"A list of questions that may be asked can be found in Chapter Four of the COLLEGE BOUND book." – Dr. Chris

ADMISSIONS DECISIONS ARE IN! ACCEPTED, WAITLISTED, DENIED...WHAT'S NEXT?

Most schools send out a letter asking you if you will accept a position on the waitlist. You can choose to accept or refuse this offer. How long you wait depends on the school's enrollment statistics. Though most students receive a decision in May or June from colleges using their waitlist, others have been known to receive acceptances a week before classes start.

The best strategy is to work with your counselor to:

- ☐ Choose and make a deposit at a good second choice.

- ☐ Get as much information from the "waitlist" college as you can.

- ☐ Let the admission office know that the college is your first choice.

- ☐ Strengthen your application, if possible.

- ☐ Offer achievements that you may not have mentioned in your application, and send new supplemental information.

- ☐ Emphasize your strong desire to attend the college, and make a case for why you're a good match. You can indicate that if accepted you'll enroll, but such a promise should be made only if you're absolutely certain.

- ☐ You can also enlist the help of an alumnus and request another (or first) interview.

- ☐ Study hard and send your final grade transcript.

- ☐ Stay involved in extracurricular activities.

NACAC Information for Wait-Listed Students

NACAC's "Statement of Students' Rights and Responsibilities in the College Admission Process" offers the following information for waitlisted students:

If you are placed on a wait list or alternate list:

- The letter that notifies you of that placement should provide a history that describes the number of students on the wait list, the number offered admission, and the availability of financial aid and housing.
- Colleges may require neither a deposit nor a written commitment as a condition of remaining on a wait list.
- Colleges are expected to notify you of the resolution of your wait list status by Aug. 1 at the latest.

Source: The National Association for College Admission Counseling
        http://www.nacacnet.org/Pages/default.aspx

TRANSFER PLANNING

Are you thinking about transferring from one college to another? Answering the following questions will help you decide your next move:

- ☐ Did you take enough time to adjust to the academics and social life at your present college? Do you understand why you are making the change – homesickness, monetary needs, family issues?

- ☐ Do you understand the transfer process to the college you would like to attend?

- ☐ Have you gotten advice from your present school? They may be able to address credit transfer issues that will be important in the admission to the next school.

- ☐ Do you have transfer plans? Does the next school have your major? What credits will transfer? Talk to your advisor.

- ☐ Have you done research on other school options? Have you found a better "fit" for you?

- ☐ Have you taken the core curriculum needed to change? Check your field of study.

- ☐ Do you meet the university's admissions policies to switch from one school environment to the next? Talk to the admissions representative at the school you're applying to. Send transcripts and test scores if applicable.

Transferring from a Community College – A Checklist

If a student is planning to transfer from a community college to a four year program, he or she should check with their advisor to see what credits will transfer. Here is a list of things to do.

- ☐ Request transcripts

- ☐ Complete school application

- ☐ Search for scholarships

- ☐ Complete departmental application if needed

- ☐ File the FAFSA online – request PIN

- ☐ Complete other financial aid forms

- ☐ Review and return financial aid award letter

- ☐ Apply and endorse loans if needed (Stafford, PLUS, private)

- ☐ Develop a budget and stick to it

ENRICHMENT OPPORTUNITIES AND SUMMER PROGRAMS

There are many opportunities in the summer for students to explore including:

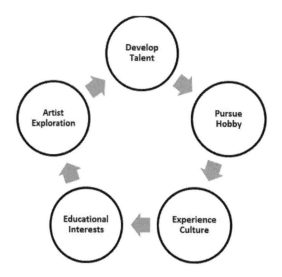

Students can also demonstrate to colleges that they have an interest in personal development outside the classroom. The cost and dates for summer programs vary greatly.

I plan to look into programs involving:

_____

_____

_____

_____

_____

_____

_____

_____

_____

_____

"In the COLLEGE BOUND book you will find HUNDREDS of live links to gap year, pre-college and summer enrichment program, volunteer and service projects, fellowships, internships and more?" – Dr. Chris

V. Special Admission Topics

This section includes the worksheets and checklists referred to in Chapter Five of COLLEGE BOUND.

"In Chapter Five of COLLEGE BOUND, you'll find detailed information and HUNDREDS of live links to specialized topics like fine arts (dramatic arts, dance, studio art, or music), athletic recruiting, the military application process, issues such as disabilities and the college search, transitioning from homeschool to college, gap year experience, and studying abroad or online." – Dr. Chris

VISUAL AND PERFORMING ARTS

Most high school students interested in the fine arts will attend liberal arts colleges with strong art and/or performing arts departments. Other students will prefer conservatories or art schools. Our recommendation is always to include several liberal arts colleges on your list even if you are primarily interested in a conservatory. This will provide you with flexibility should you change your mind about your educational plans before the end of your senior year; it also helps ensure that you will have college options, since conservatory and art school admissions are hard to predict.

RECRUITED ATHLETES

Athletic talent can provide opportunities for student athletes in the college search process. While it can present unique advantages for students, it also can bring unique challenges.

MILITARY OPTIONS

Every year thousands of young men and women make the choice to serve their country. They enjoy a military career by enlisting in one of the following branches: Air Force, Army, Coast Guard, Marines, Navy, U.S. Merchant Marine Academy, and National Guard. Some individuals will apply directly to a four year service academy such as U.S. Military Academy-West Point, New York; U.S. Naval Academy in Annapolis, Maryland; the Air Force Academy in Denver, Colorado; and the Coast Guard Academy in Groton, Connecticut. Completing your education in one of these programs will earn you a bachelor's degree, commissioned reserve officer status, and a commitment to the military for a number of years. Another option is applying to a Reserve Officers' Training Corps (ROTC) scholarship program at a college. These are two, three, and four year scholarship programs which help you decide which direction you would like to pursue (ROTC College Profiles).

http://www.airforce.com/

http://www.goarmy.com/#/?channel=careers&marquee=strongStories

http://www.uscg.mil/default.asp; http://www.marines.mil/Pages/Default.aspx

http://www.navy.mil/swf/index.asp; http://www.usmma.edu/;

http://www.arng.army.mil/Pages/Default.aspx

http://www.collegeprofiles.com/rotc.html

THE COLLEGE SEARCH FOR STUDENTS WITH DISABILITIES

All colleges and universities, public and private, are required by the American with Disabilities Act (ADA) to provide support and access to programs, services, and facilities. Most schools have disability offices to answer questions prospective and attending students may have.

A student with a documented learning disability (LD) may choose to disclose his or her LD to colleges. In cases where disclosing an LD may help a college more accurately interpret the student's transcript, it might be beneficial. A student should discuss his or her specific circumstances with his or her counselors. Colleges are required by law to accommodate students with disabilities, but it is helpful to know what types of accommodations the college offers.

Here are several tips for students with disabilities:

☐ Documentation of your disabilities with letters from your physician(s), counselors, therapists, case managers, school psychologist, and other service providers such as teachers, may be needed.

☐ Letters of recommendation from teachers, coaches, mentors, family, and friends can be helpful.

☐ Read and understand the federal laws that apply to students with disabilities.

☐ Do your research for support groups and advocacy approaches.

☐ Visit campuses – living conditions, support services, classroom support, and campus lifestyle.

☐ Ask about orientation programs especially for students with disabilities—check to see if you need to register early for classes.

☐ Ask about an individualized education program (IEP).

☐ Check out what the school offers in the way of technology – voice synthesizers, voice recognition, and /or visual learning instruments.

☐ Does the school offer intramural activities/social activities?

☐ Learn the entire layout of the campus – are all buildings easily accessible? Be realistic; a hilly campus may not be the best choice no matter what accommodations they have.

Questions might include the following:

- ☐ What type of support is available for students with learning disabilities?

- ☐ Is the program monitored by a full-time professional staff?

- ☐ Has the program been evaluated, and if so, by whom?

- ☐ Are there any concerns for the program's future?

- ☐ Who counsels students with learning disabilities during registration, orientation, and course selection?

- ☐ How does the school propose to help with the specific disability?

- ☐ Which courses provide tutoring?

- ☐ What kind of tutoring is available, and who does it—peers or staff?

- ☐ Is tutoring automatic, or must the student request assistance?

- ☐ How well do faculty members accept students with learning disabilities?

- ☐ May students with learning disabilities take a lighter load?

- ☐ Are courses in study skills or writing skills offered?

- ☐ Have counselors who work with students with learning disabilities received special training? Whom can you contact if you have concerns during the academic year?

- ☐ How do students on campus spend their free time? May students with learning disabilities take more time to graduate?

HOMESCHOOLED – NAVIGATING THE NEXT STEP

Is the Application Process Different for Homeschooled Students?

Colleges view applications from homeschooled students differently. Therefore, it is important for students to take more time with their application process.

- ☐ Take the college preparatory curriculum and build your transcript portfolio.

- ☐ Check deadlines and dates.

- ☐ Create a resume of your extracurricular activities.

- ☐ Ask for recommendations from those who know you well.

- ☐ Speak with each college about your situation and learn what schools are homeschool friendly— they will want to see a letter of completion and transcript of grades.

- ☐ Take the standardized test such as the SAT or ACT with Writing plus the SAT Subject Area tests.

- ☐ Go on a college interview if offered.

- ☐ Apply for financial aid if needed.

- ☐ Placement testing may be required prior to registration.

- ☐ Check out sites online such as Home School Friendly Colleges - http://homeschoolfriendlycolleges.com/.

- ☐ If you want to play college athletics, review this website: Home School Legal Defense Association - http://www.hslda.org/.

- ☐ Interested in the arts? Be sure to meet the requirements and deadlines for portfolios and auditions.

"GAP YEAR," VOLUNTEERISM, AND STUDY ABROAD

According to the University of Delaware, the definition of "Gap Year" is a "temporary position (1 – 3 years) between college, graduate school and/or a full time job." Many students are interested in "taking a year off" before buckling down to a "serious" job or graduate school. These temporary "in-the-meantime" jobs can provide experience, direction, emotional and cognitive growth, and satisfy curiosity about the real world. Do you have an interest in travel, learning new languages, making new friends, volunteering, taking a gap year, developing ideas, and facing challenges? A list of gap year resource websites can be found in the **COLLEGE BOUND** book.

STUDY ABROAD CHECKLIST

Study abroad can be an exciting and life changing experience, so begin by planning ahead. The following checklist will help you remember some important things that need to be done before you depart.

- ☐ Apply early enough for a new passport or to renew an old one, and do the same for your student visa.

- ☐ Get a complete physical, including immunizations. It's a good idea to have a copy of your medical records sent ahead of time to your study abroad program.

- ☐ Fill prescriptions.

- [ ] Meet with your academic counselor for a review before taking your trip.

- [ ] Be sure necessary financial aid documents are complete including scholarship applications, loan applications, and FAFSA renewal.

- [ ] If you will be away from the first of the year through April 15, complete and file your tax return early.

- [ ] Make multiple copies of important documents – one for yourself, one for your parents, and one for your study abroad program administrators. Include credit cards, passport, insurance information, etc.

- [ ] Make a list of important phone numbers, addresses, and other contact information. Put a copy in with your important document packages (see above).

- [ ] Check out international phone cards and cell phones.

- [ ] Bring enough converted currency for the first few days in your new country.

NOTES

NOTES

VI. Financial Aid/Scholarships

This section includes the worksheets and checklists referred to in Chapter Six of COLLEGE BOUND.

"Chapter Six of COLLEGE BOUND includes all the basics about financial aid and scholarships, and detailed information about other types of aid such as grants, work study, loans, etc. Do your homework and find the best options available. And remember – do NOT pay for scholarship searches – you can do them yourself for free, and the HUNDREDS of links provided in the COLLEGE BOUND book is a great place to start." – Dr. Chris

GET THE BASICS—FINANCIAL AID 101

What It Costs: See the Big Picture

Many students worry that tuition and the other costs of continuing their education will be out of reach, but don't let the price tag stop you. It's only part of the picture. Keep in mind the major benefits of investing in your education.

Most students receive some kind of financial aid to help pay for the cost of their education. A few students even get a "free ride," where all their costs are paid for. With determination and assistance from financial aid, you can make the education you dream about a reality. Use this section to learn how.

Who Gives Aid

Scholarships	Grants	Work-study Assistance	Low-interest Loans

▲

State governments, schools, employers, individuals, private companies, nonprofits, religions groups, and professional organization

The U.S. Department of Education should be your first source to access financial aid.

Who it is for: See if You are Eligible

☐ You might be eligible if all of these apply to you:

☐ You are a U.S. citizen or eligible noncitizen.

☐ You are a high school graduate or GED holder.

☐ You are working toward a degree or certificate in an eligible program.

You are not in default on a federal student loan and do not owe money to the government, related to other grants or loans.

Applying for Federal Aid: Meet the FAFSA

☐ Get free information and help from your school counselor, the financial aid office at the college or career aid office at the college or career school you plan to attend, or the US Department of Education at www.federalstudentaid.ed.gov or 1-800-4-FED-AID (1-800-433-3243). Free help is available any time during the application process.

☐ You should never have to pay for help. Get a Federal Student Aid PIN, a personal identification number. A PIN lets you apply, "sign" your online Free Application for Federal Student Aid (FAFSA)), make corrections to your application information and more –so keep safe. Go to http://www.pin.ed.gov.

☐ Collect the documents needed to apply, including income tax returns and W-2 forms (and other records of income). A full list of what you need is at http://www.fafsa.ed.gov. Tax return not completed at the time you apply? Estimate the tax information, apply, and correct information later.

☐ Complete the FAFSA between Jan. 1 and June 30 (no exceptions to either date!). Apply as soon as possible after Jan. 1 to meet schools and state aid deadlines (see note at bottom of page.) Apply online (the faster and easier way) by going to www.fafsa.ed.gov. If you don't already have your PIN, you can get it when you complete online. FAFSA.ED will send you your Student Aid Report (SAR) – the result of your FAFSA.

☐ ED will send you your Student Aid Report (SAR) – the result of your FAFSA. Review your SAR, and if necessary, make changes or corrections and submit your SAR for reprocessing. Your complete, correct SAR will contain your Expected Family Contribution (EFC) – the number used to determine your federal student aid eligibility.

☐ Your college might request additional information from you. Be sure to respond by the deadlines, or you might not receive federal student aid.

All applicants: Contact the financial aid office if you have questions about the aid being offered.

First time applicants: Review award letters from schools to compare amounts and types of aid being offered. Decide which school to attend based on a combination of (a) how well the school suits your needs; and (b) its affordability after all aid is taken into account.

Note: You also might be able to get financial aid from your state government, your school, or a private scholarship. Research non-federal aid early (ideally, start in the spring of your junior year of high school). Be sure to meet all application deadlines.

Completing the FAFSA: Do It Online

It's recommended that you complete the FAFSA online. More help is available online, and you'll get a response within 3-5 days, rather than 2-3 weeks by mail.

What You Pay: Understand the EFC

The aid you qualify for depends on your Expected Family Contribution, or EFC. The EFC is a number that schools use to determine how much federal aid you would receive if you attended that school.

When you apply for federal student aid, you will be asked to provide information about you and/or your family's finances, such as income, assets, and family size. After you submit the application, you will receive an EFC based on this information.

Your contribution may come from a combination of savings, income, and loans.

FAFSA4Caster: Be Ahead of the Curve

If you are a high school junior, *http://www.FAFSA4Caster.com* can help you estimate how much federal assistance you might receive. This FREE tool helps you:

- ☐ Estimate your eligibility for federal student aid.
- ☐ Reduce the time it takes to complete the FAFSA.
- ☐ Plan for your future financial needs.

What Aid Covers

There are five basic costs associated with going to college. Financial aid may be used for:

Room and Board	Tuition and Fees	Personal Expenses	Travel	Books and Suppies

GLOSSARY OF FINANCIAL AID TERMS

Financial aid has its own vocabulary. Here are the most commonly used terms and acronyms.

Award Letter - Issued by a college's financial aid office, this is the official notification of financial aid a student is eligible to receive.

Alternative loans - Loans are available to any student and generally a co-signer is needed. Credit score and debt-to-income ratio are factors in determining the approval of an alternative loan. There are many alternative loan programs available.

Bursar - This college office handles both the distribution of financial aid and the payment of fees and tuition. The Bursar may also be called financial officer, or something similar.

Cost of Attendance (COA) - This is the total amount it will cost a student to attend a particular college. It includes tuition, housing and meals, fees, books, supplies, transportation costs, and personal expenses.

CSS Profile - The CSS Profile (https://profileonline.collegeboard.com/prf/index.jspis) a secondary financial aid form provided by the College Board that the colleges use to help the colleges determine if the student is eligible for money. The CSS Profile should be filed early in October while the FAFSA should be completed on or after January 1 in order to receive early information regarding your status for financial aid.

Equal Opportunity - Colleges are committed to assuring equal opportunity with respect to both education and employment and do not discriminate on the basis of race, color, religion, age, national origin, gender, or disability. This complies with Title IV of the Civil Rights Act of 1964, Title IX of the Educational Amendments of 1973, and other applicable statutes.

Expected Family Contribution (EFC) - This is the amount that the federal government estimates that a family *should* be able to pay toward the cost of a child's education. This information is compiled from the FAFSA by the federal government. In many instances, the EFC (http://www.fafsa.ed.gov/help/fftoc01g.htm) is calculated without taking into consideration any unexpected changes in income (not shown by the results from taxes) or other emergencies.

FAFSA - FAFSA (http://www.fafsa.ed.gov/) is the standard form from the Department of Education that determines eligibility for all state and federal grants. Generally, you must fill this out before a college can begin processing your request for financial aid. Apply as early as possible beginning January 1st of each year. Schools and states have their own deadlines. Contact them for exact deadline dates. Current tax information will be needed to complete the form fully.

Federal Academic Competitive Grant (ACG) – Also known as the Federal ACG (http://studentaid.ed.gov/PORTALSWebApp/students/english/NewPrograms.jsp) is available to students who are U.S. citizens, Pell Grant eligible, registered full-time (either freshman or sophomore) and completed a "rigorous" high school program.

Federal Community Service Work-Study Program - This program is a partnership between the federal government and the college. It's based on financial need according to a student's completed FAFSA. This program is meant to place eligible students in the community as volunteers. Although students may volunteer for an organization, they're paid. The positions are primarily off campus. U.S. citizenship or eligible non-citizenship status is required.

Federal Pell Grant - The Federal Pell Grant (http://www.ed.gov/programs/fpg/index.html) is available to students who qualify by completing the FAFSA. The award can be as much as $4,731 per year and is determined by the Expected Family Contribution (EFC). These government grants are awarded to students who need a great deal of financial aid. They do not need to be repaid.

Federal PLUS Loan - Parents may borrow under the Federal Direct Plus Loan Program (http://studentaid.ed.gov/PORTALSWebApp/students/english/parentloans.jspon) behalf of the student. Parents are eligible to borrow the cost of education minus aid based on credit-worthiness. Government-subsidized loans are limited to the cost of education. Parents do not need to demonstrate need. Interest rates can vary.

Federal Stafford Loan - Stafford Loans http://www.staffordloan.com/ are available to all students who complete the FAFSA. There are two categories of a Federal Stafford Loan: subsidized and unsubsidized. With a subsidized loan, the government pays the interest while the student is in college. With an unsubsidized loan, the student is responsible for interest while in college. Payments for Federal Stafford Loans usually begin six months after the student drops below six credit hours or after graduation.

Federal Direct Stafford Loan limits –
First Years' - $3,500 / Sophomores - $4,500 / Juniors/Seniors - $5,500

Please note: An additional $2,000 in unsubsidized loans is available for all students. Independent First Year students and sophomores may qualify for an additional $4,000 in unsubsidized loans. Juniors and seniors may qualify for an additional $5,000 in unsubsidized loans.

Federal Supplemental Education Opportunity Grant (SEOG) - The Federal SEOG http://studentaid.ed.gov/PORTALSWebApp/students/english/FSEOG.jsp is available to students who qualify by being eligible for the Federal Pell Grant. Up to $600 per year.

Federal Work-Study Program – There are funds for the Federal Work-Study Program http://www2.ed.gov/programs/fws/index.html available from the federal government. Students are awarded federal work-study money based on their financial need as determined by the completed FAFSA. Students must be U.S. citizens or eligible non-citizens to receive these funds.

Financial Aid Package – This is an offer of money for a student from a college. Can consist of several kinds of aid, including loans, grants, campus jobs, and may or may not include scholarships. This package fills the gap between parent's contribution and total cost of college.

Free Application for Federal Student Aid (FAFSA) - This is the form a student completes to determine the EFC and the financial aid that will be available.

Grants and Scholarships - Grants and scholarships constitute free money available for education through a college or university, the state, the federal government, and outside agencies. Grants and scholarships may be awarded on the basis of need, GPA, merit, or all three. http://www.students.gov/STUGOVWebApp/Public?topicID=15&operation=topic)

Interest - Interest is the amount charged by a bank for the use of its money through the life of a loan.

Independent Status Student - Independent students can file their FAFSA independently of their parents. To qualify, you must meet one of the requirements below:

☐ You have reached your 24th birthday before January 1st of the beginning of the academic year for which you are applying for financial aid.

☐ You are married.

☐ You have children who received more than half of their support from you.

☐ You have dependents (other than your children or spouse) that live with you and who will receive more than half of their support from you, now through June 30th of the end of the academic year for which you are applying for financial aid.

☐ You are an orphan or ward of the court (or were a ward of the court until 18 or certified as being homeless).

☐ You are a veteran of the U.S. Armed Forces.

Merit Scholarships - Merit money (http://www.meritaid.com/) given to students on the basis of demonstrated ability—academic, performance, service, athletics, etc. It is not based on need, and does not need to be repaid. Most scholarships come from colleges themselves and vary widely from institution to institution. There are also some scholarships available from businesses, alumni organizations, and programs like the National Merit Scholarship.

Student Employment Program (SEP) - This is work—either on or off campus—for students to help them pay for their education.

Work Study - A campus job may be offered as part of a financial aid package. These usually require 15-20 hours a week on campus and usually allow the student to do some studying while working. Examples might include monitoring a welcome desk in university office or working at a library desk.

LEARN WHAT'S AVAILABLE — SCHOLOARHIPS, GRANTS, LOANDS AND MORE...

Scholarships: "Earn to Learn"

Scholarships are gifts. They don't need to be repaid. Some scholarships are merit based. You earn them by meeting or exceeding certain standards set by the scholarship-giver. They might be awarded based on academic achievement, or a combination of academics and a special talent, trait, or interest. Awards are also available for students who are interested in particular fields of study, who are members of underrepresented groups, who live in certain areas of the country, or who demonstrate financial need. Scholarships may be offered by:

- ☐ Schools
- ☐ Employers
- ☐ Individuals
- ☐ Private Companies

- ☐ Nonprofits
- ☐ Religious Groups
- ☐ Professional and Social Organizations

Most scholarship applications ask for information such as year in school, citizenship, state of residence, religion, ethnic background, disability, military status, employer, and membership organizations. An application requires information on extracurricular activities, sports, leadership, career plans, major plans, and future goals.

Where Do I Look for Scholarships?

- ☐ Internet Scholarships

☐ High School Counselor's Office

☐ Public Library

☐ College's Financial Aid Office

☐ Bookstores - Financial Aid Guides

☐ Organizations - religious, military, community service agencies, unions, professional associations

☐ Employers

☐ College Aid Offices

☐ State Scholarship Programs

Steps in Your Search for Money to Pay for College

☐ Begin your search early, write down the deadlines, and fill out scholarship applications ahead of time.

☐ Use all resources available from the colleges themselves, internet sources, community, regional, and national sources.

☐ Know your focus. If you are seeking undergraduate scholarship opportunities, do not focus on the graduate level.

☐ Follow all the steps and instructions. Ignoring details could ruin your chances to have your application reviewed. Neatness counts.

☐ Write an essay that makes a strong impression about you personally.

☐ Check the address to be sure it gets where it needs to go. Keep a backup file in case it is needed.

☐ Project yourself as confident and courteous. Reveal the importance of assistance while being respectful.

☐ Have a friend, teacher, or parent review the application and essay before you send it via email or mail it. Ask for help if you need as needed.

How Do I Avoid Scholarship Scams?

There are several ways scams become apparent. Finaid.org http://www.finaid.org/scholarships/common.phtml discusses several including:

- [ ] If you must pay money to get money, it might be a scam.

- [ ] If it sounds too good to be true, it probably is.

- [ ] Spend the time, not the money.

- [ ] Never invest more than a postage stamp to get information about scholarships.

- [ ] Nobody can guarantee that you'll win a scholarship.

- [ ] Legitimate scholarship foundations do not charge application fees.

- [ ] If you're suspicious of an offer, it's usually with good reason.

Grants: Need and Receive

Grants are also gifts, but they're usually based on financial need. Most often, grant aid comes from federal and state governments and individual colleges.

- [ ] TEACH Grant for students planning to teach low income students

- [ ] Pell Grants

- [ ] Academic Competitiveness Grants

- [ ] FSEOG

- [ ] Federal Educational Opportunity Grants

- [ ] National SMART Grant- Math, Technology, Foreign Language, Physical and Computer

Loans: Borrow for the Future

FEDERAL STUDENT LOANS AND PRIVATE LOANS: Loans are a contract to borrow money and repay it over time, with interest. In the case of most federal student loans, you do not need to begin repaying them until several months after you leave college or are no longer enrolled at least half-time.

Work-Study: Get a Job

The Federal Work-Study (FWS) program provides part-time jobs for students with financial need to help them pay for their education. The program is administered by participating schools. It's designed to put you to work in the community, or in a job related to your studies, whenever possible.

Tools and Tips: Find and Save Money

On the next page are a few tips to get started. Look at:

Federal Student Aid Scholarship Website	Merit or non-need based scholarshipos for academically talented student	Athletic, Arts or Military Scholarships
State Education Agency	Instate Resident Scholarhips	Live at Home/Community college - transfer to four year college

HOW CAN I SAVE FOR MY CHILD'S COLLEGE EDUCATION?

Your child is focused on their school work, activities, and developing interests while you begin to focus on the end goal, your child's entrance into college. Talking to a financial planner at your local bank is a great place to start to look at:

- ☐ 529 Savings Plans

- ☐ Stock and Mutual Funds

- ☐ Inheritance and Grandparents

- ☐ Universal Life Insurance

- ☐ Certificates of Deposits

- ☐ Bonds and Zero-coupons Bonds

- ☐ Independent College 500-Indexed Certificates of Deposit

NEED-BASED VERSUS MERIT-BASED FINANCIAL AID

It is important to understand how to get the most money from the colleges a student is applying to, as aid can be need-based or merit-based.

Need-Based Aid is based on the family's financial need. A family can figure this amount to be the Cost of Attendance (COA) form the Expected Family Income (EFC).

Merit-Based Aid is usually awarded for a student's academic achievement in high school, for special talents such as music or athletics, often awarded by states, colleges, universities, private groups or individuals, or by tuition waivers.

KEEP TRACK OF COLLEGE COSTS

Expenses	College 1	College 2	College 3	College 4
Tuition and fees:				
In-state	$	$	$	$
Out-of-State	$	$	$	$
Books and supplies	$	$	$	$
Room and board	$	$	$	$
Transportation	$	$	$	$
Miscellaneous	$	$	$	$
Total Expenses:	$	$	$	$
Funds Available:				
Student and parent contributions	$	$	$	$
Grants:				
Federal – Stafford Loans; Perkins Loans;	$	$	$	$
Graduate PLUS; Parent PLUS	$	$	$	$
Local:				
Institute (College or University)	$	$	$	$
Scholarships: Athletic, Arts, ROTC, Military				
1)	$	$	$	$
2)	$	$	$	$
3)	$	$	$	$
Private Student Loans	$	$	$	$
Summer Earnings	$	$	$	$
Loans	$	$	$	$
529 Savings Plan	$	$	$	$
Total Funds, Grants, Loans, Scholarships, Work-study available	$	$	$	$
Funding Gap between College Costs and Financial Aid	$	$	$	$

Are your "funds available" less than or equal to your total for "expenses?" If not, you have a funding gap which means that you have more expenses than funds available and will need to take out a loan or seek other sources of funds.

SAMPLE AWARD REPORT

Mr. Samuel Sample
123 Sample St.
Sampleville, ST 99999

Dear Samuel:

Congratulations on your admission to Sample University. We in Student Financial Aid look forward to working with you and your family over the next four years. We have reviewed your application for financial aid for the 2011-2012 academic year and are pleased to make this tentative offer of financial aid assistance based on a careful analysis of the information you provided.

Your need was calculated using the Budget and Resources detailed below:

Budget Category	Amount
Tuition and fees	39,212
Room and meals	11,234
Books and personal	2,764
Travel	400

Budget totals	53,610

Resources	Amount
Student contribution	1,900
Parental contribution	9,760

Total Resources	11,660
Need (Budget - Resources)	**41,950**

To meet your need, Sample University offers you the following assistance:

Source	Fall	Spring	Total
Sample U Scholarship	18,225	18,225	36,450
Self Help Offer		2,750	2,750	5,500
Total Awards	20,975	20,975	41,950

The above financial aid award is tentative pending receipt of the following items:

Sample University Student Information Review Form - As a Sample University Scholarship recipient, you must complete the Student Information Review Form before your scholarship can be credited to your student account. The online form is now available on Web at student.sampleu.edu under the "for Students" section in "Financial Record." You must have a current valid certificate on your computer in order to access the form.

The questionnaire helps us determine if you match any of the named scholarships which are used to fund students' Sample U financial aid. The form asks questions about your personal interests, extracurricular activities and work experience, as well as your plans during your time at Sample University. Scholarship aid is made possible by a community of alums and friends whose generosity allows the Institute to maintain a policy of need-blind admissions. The information that you share enables us to show donors the impact of their philanthropy. If you have questions or experience any difficulty with accessing or completing this form, please contact finaid@sampleu.edu.

Please feel free to contact Student Financial Aid at 000/000-0000 with any questions regarding your financial aid award or visit our web site at http://web.sampleu.edu/sfs/.

Sincerely,

Student Financial Services

HOW DO I APPEAL MY FINANCIAL AWARD?

Congratulations, you were admitted to your college of your dreams! Next you receive a letter of notification from the financial aid/scholarships office. If you did not receive the award you expected, you may need to make an appeal. You won't know what is possible until you ask. Follow these steps to appeal for more funds.

- ☐ Contact the aid office and ask them what procedure you should follow to appeal for more financial assistance. Visit the office in person if time is on your side.

- ☐ A "financial appeal" is when you attempt to demonstrate that with your current level of income and assets, you can't afford to pay the total cost of attendance for the first year. Ask the aid counselor to recalculate the initial Expected Family Contribution (EFC). Be sure to share any new information as well as all supporting documents including income verification, an update on asset holdings, a list of unusually high expenses, a description of special circumstances, etc. This new data could bring your EFC more in line with what you can afford.

- ☐ A "competitive appeal" is based on the rivalry that can exist between schools when they are roughly a similar selective admissions basis. Ask if the school has an institutional policy and sufficient scholarship funds, that "puts them on record" as willing to respond to the aid packages of their rivals. Sharing copies of the other award letter with the intent of improving your original aid award may be a way to substantiate a competitive appeal.

BE MONEY SMART – GET THE MOST "BANG FOR YOUR BUCK!"

Money Management Tips: Spend with Care

- ☐ Make a budget and stick to it.

- ☐ Avoid credit cards.

- ☐ Buy used books.

- ☐ Leave your car at home.

- ☐ Watch the ATM fees.

Bad Deals and Scams: Know and Avoid Them

☐ Fee-based scholarship searches. Bad deal!

☐ Fee-based FAFSA assistance. Bad deal! Lots of free help is available to help you fill out the FAFSA.

☐ Protect your identity. Avoid scams. As you go through the financial aid application process, to reduce risk:

- o After completing your FAFSA online, exit application and close browser.

- o Don't tell anyone your Federal Student Aid PIN, even the person helping you fill out the application.

- o Review your financial aid documents and keep track of the amounts you applied for and received.

- o Never give personal information over the phone or Internet unless you made the contact. For questions about a solicitation or your student loan account, call 1-800-4-FED-AID.

- o Shred receipts and documents with personal information when you are finished with them.

- o Immediately report lost or stolen identification to the issuer and to the police. Report fraud and identity theft. For more information about financial aid fraud or to report fraud, visit the Federal Trade Commission's scholarship scams page http://www.ftc.gov/bcp/edu/microsites/scholarship/index.shtml. If you suspect that your student information has been stolen, contact one of these resources immediately:

  - ▪ U.S. Department of Education, 1-800-MIS-USED (1-800-647-8733)

  - ▪ Federal Trade Commission, 1-800-ID-THEFT (1-877-438-4338)

Other Considerations

Private loans. Private loans can be useful, but watch out for bad deals. Check with the Better Business Bureau (http://www.bbb.org/us/) - *Source: U.S. Department of Education*

THE ULTIMATE BUDGET WORKSHEET FOR COLLEGE STUDENTS

CATEGORY	MONTHLY BUDGET	MONTHLY ACTUAL	SEMESTER BUDGET	SEMESTER ACTUAL	SCHOOL YR BUDGET	SCHOOL YR ACTUAL
INCOME						
From Jobs						
From Parents						
From Student Loans						
From Scholarships						
From Financial Aid						
Miscellaneous Income						
EXPENSES						
Rent or Room & Board						
Utilities						
Telephone						
Groceries						
Car Payment/Transportation						
Insurance						
Gasoline/Oil						
Entertainment						
Eating Out/Vending						
Tuition						
Books						
School Fees						
Computer Expense						
Miscellaneous Expense						
NET INCOME (Income less Expenses)						

If an expense is incurred more or less often than monthly, convert it to a monthly amount when calculating the monthly budget amount. For instance, auto expense that is billed every six months would be converted to monthly by dividing the six month premium by six.

NOTES

VII. Heading Off to College: The Transition

This section includes the worksheets and checklists referred to in Chapter Seven of COLLEGE BOUND.

"In COLLEGE BOUND you will find a number of live links to cheap textbooks, study tips and learning styles, and how to smooth your transition from high school to college." – Dr. Chris

Heading off to college is exciting and nerve-wracking at the same time! "Did I choose the right college?" "Did I pick the right dorm?" "What if I don't get along with my roommate?" "How do I sign up for classes" "What do I need to pack?" And lastly, "How will I say 'goodbye' to family and friends?" These questions and more will be answered in time, and the tips below can help.

PACKING THE ESSENTIALS

It's never too early to start shopping for the essentials. You can start early by getting any seasonal items as soon as possible. Know the layout of your room. Find out what you can bring and what you can't bring. Some schools allow small refrigerators, but not microwaves. Call your roommate ahead of time so you don't duplicate items. Buy in bulk when you can. Bring your own "munchies."

What to Take...

- ☐ Sheets, mattress pad, towels, pillow, and comforter.

- ☐ Bathroom supplies including shampoo, deodorant, soap, toothpaste and brush, flip-flops, other personal toiletries, and cleaning supplies.

- ☐ Bean bags, futons, rug, curtains, lighting and bulbs, and an alarm clock.

- ☐ Small storage containers, a backpack, a bucket, a bulletin board with pins; desk items - stapler, pens, pencils, paper, binders, paper clips; message board, ruler, notebooks, trash can, binders, book ends, calculator, and index cards.

- ☐ First aid kit, medicines, "munchies," coffee cups, and travel mugs.

- ☐ Laundry basket, laundry detergent, stain-remover, fabric softener, Goo-Gone, rolls of quarters, sewing kit, portable vacuum, iron and board, and a lint brush.

- ☐ TV, microwave, small refrigerators, batteries, iron, flashlight, dinnerware, cups, glasses and utensils, and a fan.

- ☐ A tool kit including duct tape, flashlight, flat head screwdriver, hammer with claw, nails, Philip's head screwdriver, pliers, wire cutters, putty knife, screws, tape measure, and a utility knife.

- ☐ Cell phones and calling cards to keep in contact with friends and family.

- ☐ Clothes for all seasons— if you don't have room, switch them out over the holidays on your visits home— appropriate shoes and boots as needed.

- ☐ Family and friends contact list for emergencies.

- ☐ Books are not cheap. You may want to shop around if you know what books are needed for the courses you plan to take.

What Not to Take…

- ☐ If freshmen are not allowed to have cars on campus at your school, you should leave your car at home. It's not always necessary to have a car on campus. Many colleges have their own shuttle buses if you are on a large campus. If you do bring a car, be aware of tow-zones, or you will find it a costly venture (around $90) to get your car back. Leave the personalized license plate home—you don't want to give strangers information about yourself.

- ☐ Hotplate burners and candles…you don't want a fire.

- ☐ All pets, high school memorabilia, or full size refrigerator.

- ☐ Expensive clothing and accessories (unfortunately it is the real world, and theft does occur).

- ☐ Jewelry you don't wear often.

- ☐ Of course, no fireworks, guns or explosives; school should be a safe place for all.

HI - TECH TOOLS – GADGETS GALORE!

Have you been thinking about what you want or need to take to college to make your life easier? Here are a few ideas of high-tech gadgets to consider for college.

- ☐ Desktop or laptop computer. Will you need special programs like an AutoCAD or Photoshop? Will you need a docking station in your dorm room? What size monitor do you need?

- ☐ Printers, scanners, fax, ink, toner cartridge replacements, and paper.

- ☐ Netbook, Notebook, Tablet, or iPad could be used in class.

- ☐ What about music? Do you have an iPod, Shuffle, Nano, Touch, or Zune, and speakers?

- ☐ Do you need to back-up your hard drives or flash drives?

- ☐ Power strips and surge protectors may be on your packing list.

- ☐ Items to have on hand – camera, extension cords, power strips, CD-Rs, back-up software, batteries, Ethernet cord, jump drive, mouse pad, wireless card, surge protectors, tools, extra-long TV cable, cell phone and charger, alarm clock, and lamps.

NOTES

SAYING GOODBYE TO HIGH SCHOOL AND HELLO TO COLLEGE LIFE

25 Tips For Incoming Freshmen

The following list includes a collection of suggestions made by upper classmen for incoming freshmen.

- ☐ Moving-in day can be stressful. Don't yell at your parents; they are trying to help you. Pack light!

- ☐ If your dorm does not have air conditioning, bring fans!

- ☐ Attend orientation activities; you will have plenty of times to do other activities later.

- ☐ Maintain contact with family and friends via email, texting, or phone calls. This will reduce his or her anxiety and fears.

- ☐ Find a balance between keeping contact with the friends from home and new friends at college.

- ☐ Don't go home every weekend. You need to establish a life on campus.

- ☐ Relationships take work to keep them going; share events to keep each other up-to-date with your lives.

- ☐ Make a good first impression and remember names.

- ☐ Find a group to sit with at lunch; get to know people in your classes; join a study group.

- ☐ Network with all types of people; you may need a recommendation for an internship or need to interview for a job in the future.

- ☐ Get to know your academic advisor to discuss your major; meet with your professors so you understand class expectations; see your RA (resident assistant) for everyday life issues; ask the registrar for help in signing up for classes and business office (bursar) for paying your bills.

- ☐ Take responsibility for your own learning.

- ☐ Study, study, study! Find a comfortable place to do your studying where you will not be disturbed.

- ☐ Ward off procrastinating when it comes to school work; attend class daily and keep organized notes. You never know what the professors will focus on in class or on exams.

☐ Get involved in activities— you never know whom you will meet or what you will enjoy. Become a leader on campus.

☐ Enjoy your weekends; you may need a break from your studies, but remember to eat right, get your exercise, get enough sleep, and stick to a calendar to meet your deadlines and appointments.

☐ Girls and Guys— stay safe, respect each other, and take care of your reputation—you are responsible for your actions.

☐ Avoid peer pressure; don't worry about what others think about you.

☐ Learn to accept change— in yourself, in others, and in situations.

☐ Maintain contact— use Facebook, Skype, or other social networking methods, but remember to be safe when interacting with strangers. Choose privacy settings carefully, change passwords often, and think before you post.

☐ Avoid "drama," gossip, and confront issues before they get too big. A word on roommates – set rules you can agree on, communicate, be considerate, be flexible, and be respectful.

☐ Don't do drugs or use alcohol illegally; they will ruin your future!

☐ Monitor spending— keep yourself on a budget—know the cost of your living, give yourself an allowance, organize receipts, be frugal, understand your debt load, avoid credit cards, and watch out for identity theft.

☐ Remember, when you go home for that first visit, you will need to talk with your parents about their expectations.

☐ Ask for help! You don't have to "go it alone." Use the power of positive thinking to accomplish your goals.

FINDING A BALANCE: STUDY SKILLS AND TIME MANAGEMENT TIPS

It is important to find a balance between classes, work, and campus activities. Remember to take your health seriously and to set realistic expectations for yourself. If you're attending classes full-time, try not to work more than 20 hours a week.

Showing up for class and having your work done on time is a great way to start your college career. There a many ways to approach the task of studying, preparing for class, and taking tests.

Study Tips

☐ Develop a schedule that meets your needs and will keep you from wandering off to other tasks.

☐ Make every hour count … so create a 24 hour a day schedule, account for sleep, class, lab time, meals, hours for study, and hours for socializing with friends and family.

☐ Keep your workspace organized so you don't spend time looking for items.

☐ Begin 30-90 minutes after a meal and never within 30 minutes of going to sleep.

☐ Study when you are alert and ready focus.

☐ Prioritize what you want to study first— rank your classes according to the assignments.

☐ Study in chunks— for 30-40 minutes at a stretch.

☐ Review your lecture notes soon after they were given to add any extra information you may remember but did not write down in your notes— take breaks at your desk so you won't get distracted. Ask yourself questions and discuss topics with peers and professors.

☐ Improve your critical thinking skills.

☐ Be the best writer you can be— most colleges have writing labs to help you with papers.

For Class

☐ Pay attention to the syllabus.

☐ Sit where you will not be distracted.

☐ For classes with recitation, i.e. foreign language, practice to sharpen skills.

☐ You can study anywhere that suits you— the library, the student lounge, your room, as long as it is conducive to learning.

☐ When reading, get the main idea, extract important details, take notes, outline text.

☐ Develop a method for note-taking— listen to lecture, formulate questions, review and revise, and research notes.

☐ Choose teachers who actively involve you in learning.

☐ See your instructors outside of class.

☐ Find a great academic or faculty advisor to work with you on your choice of courses.

Taking Tests

☐ Taking exams—glance at the test and then always read the directions.

☐ Answer the easy questions first, pick out key words for true false statements like "always" and "never"; in multiple choice questions, eliminate the obvious wrong answers first and choose from the rest.

☐ Essay questions— pay attention to the instructor's words such as "list," "describe, or "compare and contrast." Do a quick outline on some scratch paper including points you want to include.

☐ Pay attention to your handwriting, grammar, punctuation, and spelling.

UNDERSTANDING YOUR LEARNING STYLE
Have you ever thought about how you learn? Your learning-style has nothing to do with intelligence; it has to do with how your brain works. There are auditory learners, tactile or kinesthetic learners, and visual learners.

"Here's a tip: Take North Carolina State's Index of Learning Styles Questionnaire to understand more about your own learning style!" – Dr. Chris

http://www.engr.ncsu.edu/learningstyles/ilsweb.html

STAYING SAFE WHILE ON CAMPUS
Read the paper, watch the news, or listen to the radio. This will alert you to crime in cities, suburbs, or in the country. No town or campus is immune from crime, so understanding what you can do to stay safe is paramount.

Many college security offices have call boxes around campus, evening escort services, and a staff that patrols day and night. Others have developed emergency alert systems that call students' cell phones. Each campus has its own reporting system.

Here are some quick tips to help ensure your safety while on campus:

☐ Walk in groups or at least with one other person – there is safety in numbers.

☐ Be aware of your surroundings—don't walk in unlit areas at night and avoid seldom-traveled shortcuts.

☐ Don't prop open entrances of residence halls – use door pass keys for safety.

☐ Keep your dorm room door locked while you're sleeping.

☐ Use door peepholes before opening your door.

- [ ] Vary your route if you walk every day to and from class, your job, or meals.

- [ ] If you're at a party, never let a stranger get a drink for you and never leave a drink unattended.

- [ ] Don't accept rides from people you don't know; a stranger may have a different agenda than you.

- [ ] Be aware of people loitering in hallways; take note of their clothes, their faces, jewelry, and unique features such as tattoos.

- [ ] Never lend your keys or identification to anyone.

- [ ] Don't leave your backpack and personal belongings unattended.

- [ ] Make sure someone knows where you are and when you expect to return.

- [ ] Consider carrying a personal alarm device, like a whistle and keep your cell phone charged.

- [ ] If you have a "gut-feeling" about a stranger, a fellow student, or a situation you find yourself in, trust your instinct and remove yourself from that situation as soon as possible.

NOTES

VIII. JUST FOR PARENTS

This section includes the worksheets and checklists referred to in Chapter Eight of COLLEGE BOUND.

"Parents need to understand their role in the admissions process, their child's role, and that of their child's counselor. The COLLEGE BOUND book expands on these issues and more." – Dr. Chris

Your children are filled with excitement as they open their letters of acceptance to the college of their dreams. You are happy for them, but you realize they are about to enter the adult world. Are they ready for what they are about to face? Have you taught them how to problem solve? Will they make good choices? This transition can be difficult for parents as well as the child. This chapter will address ways to support your children as they navigate through the application process, ways to support your children as they make the transition to college, and ways to adjust to the "empty nest."

WHAT PARENTS NEED TO KNOW ABOUT HANDLING THE ADMISSIONS PROCESS

It is important to understand your role in the admissions process as well as your child's and his or her counselor's roles.

Parent/Guardian Support is Important in the College Planning Process

- ☐ Understand that each child is unique.

- ☐ Recognize that students live in a complex time that is often highly competitive.

- ☐ Respect your child's choices and listen with an open mind.

- ☐ Provide helpful, encouraging, and constructive feedback.

- ☐ Model appropriate behavior; they copy what they observe.

- ☐ Encourage children to communicate with the colleges directly; try not to take over the process or the responsibilities that are the applicants.

- ☐ Remember that college counselors are professionals who have unique experiences in this field.

- ☐ If you are perplexed by a counselor's suggestion – ask the person to clarify the recommendations.

☐ Do not assume that online blogs and social networks have accurate admission information.

What to Expect From Your Child

☐ Your children should develop their skills to research, to make their own decisions by understanding their values, interests, and work ethic.

☐ Timely attention to all tasks and deadlines through the college application cycle.

☐ Honest and open communication; open-mindedness; a willingness to be assertive, and ask questions.

☐ Openness to allowing parents and guardians to assist them in owning the search and application process.

What to Expect From Counselors Who Are Professionals in this Field

☐ Expert guidance and support through the admissions process.

☐ Assistance in creating a thoughtful and realistic application list.

☐ Clearly identified tasks for parents and students to complete.

☐ Thoughtful consideration of counselor recommendation comments

☐ A willingness for the parent or guardian to assist the child in owning the process by helping him or her learn to be self-reliant and self-sufficient

STAYING ORGANIZED

It will be important to stay organized as you proceed through the college application process. Here are some tips to make life easier:

☐ Create a filing system that works for you.

☐ Purchase folders and labels to hold information on applications, bank accounts, copies of checks and payment stubs, important college information, correspondence, housing data, insurance (car and medical), expenses (including travel and tuition).

☐ Keep track of contacts at each institution.

☐ Making a calendar that spans the school year will keep you focused on important dates such as orientation, the start of classes, Parent's Weekend, holiday breaks, the start of the next semester, the end of the school year, and when tuition is due.

Keep track of the following pertinent data:

- [ ] Health forms

- [ ] Date of Physical

- [ ] Vaccinations

- [ ] Nearest Pharmacy – address and phone number

- [ ] Phone number of Health Center at College

- [ ] Address and phone of hospital closest to college

- [ ] Child's blood type

- [ ] Eyeglass prescription

- [ ] Other medication prescriptions

- [ ] Medical Waiver

- [ ] Housing Forms – questionnaire, housing preference

- [ ] Tuition bills and New Student Orientation – books, supplies, and other miscellaneous expenses

- [ ] Bank information – address, account number, ABA routing number, transfer information, credit card expectations

- [ ] Power of Attorney and Other Written Consents in case of emergencies such as hospitalization, insurance needs, and/or treatment by physicians

HEALTH AND INSURANCE

Will your insurance cover your child's medical care away from home? Be sure to inquire with your insurance company to insure coverage. Can prescriptions be filled out of state?

Your child should be prepared to handle the basics of first aid. Be sure he or she has the following on hand:

- [ ] Acetaminophen or ibuprofen for aches, pains, and fever

- [ ] Rubbing Alcohol and hydrogen peroxide

- [ ] Antibacterial and antibiotic ointments

- [ ] Bandages or all sizes – first aid tape and scissors

- [ ] Cough drops and syrup

- [ ] Eye drops

☐ Hot and cold packs

☐ Medicine for allergies, colds, diarrhea

☐ Thermometer

☐ Tweezers

☐ Antacids for upset stomach

Be sure your child knows how to avoid staph and other infections by:

☐ Frequently washing his or her hands

☐ Not sharing personal items

☐ Keeping cuts and scrapes covered by clean bandages

Insurance documentation should be on record including health policy numbers, car insurance policy numbers, as well as Homeowner's or Renter's Insurance to cover losses due to damage from water, smoke, theft, or mechanical breakdown. Be sure to take an inventory of the property that was taken to college.

<table>
<tr><td>NOTES</td></tr>
<tr><td></td></tr>
</table>

THE MONEY DISCUSSION

It is important to discuss finances with your child. Is your child ready for responsible spending within a budget?

☐ Make a budget.

☐ Open a credit card for emergencies.

☐ Open a checking account. Be sure your child knows how to write a check, make a deposit, keep a register, reconcile statements, and address risks of identity theft.

☐ Find out if a direct deposit or money transfer can occur at a bank near or on campus. Does the bank have an ATM, and does it charge a fee to use it?

☐ Explain the difference between a debit and credit card. Discuss monthly service charges, fees for "bounced" checks, or perks from the bank.

☐ Keeping receipts and deposit slips in a safe place is important so your children can balance their checkbooks.

☐ Do they need access to a savings account? Can transfers be made online?

☐ Are students aware of other types of accounts such as Money Markets or CDs?

NEW STUDENT ORIENTATION

Has your child received his or her new student orientation information? Do you need to register, respond or make a payment? Are hotel reservations made and dorm rooms ready for moving in? Have you arranged for transportation to college? There are many benefits for students who attend orientation programs put on by the college and universities. They are designed to:

☐ Assist students in the transition into college.

☐ Provide the students with an opportunity to familiarize themselves with the campus, dorm rooms, classrooms, dining halls, library, bookstores, computer services, laundry facilities, publications, stores, etc.

☐ Help students understand what support services are available such as an infirmary, counseling and career services, writing centers, religious centers, etc.

☐ Meet their roommate(s).

☐ Meet other students in their classes as well as upper classmen.

☐ Discuss students' accounts and register for classes.

☐ Explain students' online accounts.

☐ Meet academic advisors to discuss goals and aspirations.

☐ Provide students with information about courses, curriculum, majors, minors, graduation requirements.

☐ Discuss extracurricular opportunities on and off campus.

☐ Provides orientation programs for parents.

☐ Introduce parent(s) to their child's new "college life."

☐ Give parents the opportunity to meet the President, Deans, and administration.

☐ Offer the opportunity for parents to ask questions.

OFF TO COLLEGE WE GO!

The drive to college leaves each person filled with anticipation and excitement, but before anyone can unpack the car, you will need to pick up the keys and other important information. Most schools will have people available to help you and your child unpack upon arrival. You will most likely unload your boxes, carry them to the dorm, move your car, and then unpack.

☐ Take note of any damages or problems in the room. Note these on the form that may be given to you by college personnel.

☐ Be creative with organization and storage space such as under the bed, on bookshelves, and in closets.

☐ Help your child create his or her workspace.

☐ Discuss dorm safety including locking doors and windows even when going to restroom.

☐ Don't overload extension cords or power outlets.

☐ Keep cell phone charged in case of emergency.

Are cars allowed on campus? Find out before your child takes a car to school. Ask yourself:

☐ Is it practical to have a car?

☐ How will you handle routine maintenance?

☐ Do you have a copy of the registration, insurance cards, and registration items?

☐ Do you have a road service plan for emergency situations?

☐ How about a second set of car keys?

☐ Does your insurance company have stipulations regarding taking the car to another state for a certain period of time?

☐ Have you located the nearest certified mechanic?

"You will find live links and a lot of information about financial aid, scholarships, student budgeting, and other topics in Chapter Eight of the COLLEGE BOUND book." – Dr. Chris

---

NOTES

What is in an emergency roadside kit?

- ☐ Car jack
- ☐ Cell phone charger
- ☐ Emergency flares, warning triangles or cones
- ☐ Fire extinguisher
- ☐ Flashlight
- ☐ Jumper cables
- ☐ Insurance and emergency numbers
- ☐ Tire inflator
- ☐ Washer fluid
- ☐ Scraper and brush for snow and ice
- ☐ Kitty litter for traction in mud and a mini shovel for snow

"What about parking? Are there certain parking lots for students? Is there a cost? Can leave the student leave their car on campus over the holidays? Know your child's travel plans whether by car, plane, or train." – Dr. Chris

Travel tips for your child:

- ☐ Photo ID
- ☐ Keep tickets in hand
- ☐ Carry keys
- ☐ Unplug electrical equipment
- ☐ Empty refrigerator of food that will spoil
- ☐ Give family itinerary
- ☐ Get spare prescriptions
- ☐ Confirm plans, flights, seat assignments
- ☐ Dress comfortably, bring food, and drink plenty of fluids
- ☐ Carry-on case no larger than 22 inches – pack light and in layers

Parents often drive off campus feeling empty. Remember, you can still send mail and care packages, join parent groups, attend athletic events and parent weekend events, make weekly phone calls, and text!

TIPS FOR ADJUSTING TO AN EMPTY NEST

Do you find yourself taking a trip down memory lane while your child's excitement builds as he or she packs the car heading off to college, starting a military career, or getting a first apartment? It is a time of change, a time to look at your child's needs and your needs. It can be a fresh beginning. Here are several tips to help you cope with this period of your life.

> *"Rest, exercise, reconnect with friends. Follow your passion. Set a schedule for communication. Take a deep breath, and start to enjoy the next phase of YOUR life!"*
> *– Dr. Chris*

IX. A Final Note

You just took a giant first step to understanding more about the college admissions process. No matter where you are in your high school career, completing **My College Bound Plan** should vastly increase your odds of getting into the college that is *the best fit for you*.

For more tips and timely information, visit www.college-path.com. Don't forget to tell your friends about the book, *COLLEGE BOUND: Proven Ways to Plan and Prepare for Getting Into the College of Your Dreams* (http://www.college-path.com/book/) and this workbook so they can get their own copies at our bookstore - http://www.college-path.com/college-path-store/- They will thank you!

Also, follow me on Twitter ID: https://twitter.com/drchristinehand; friend the College Path fan page on Facebook: http://www.facebook.com/pages/College-Pathcom/74842441589 and subscribe to College-Path.com's RSS Feed: http://feeds.feedburner.com/CollegePath for the latest information.

Lastly, special acknowledgments go to contributors to this workbook including the U.S. Department of Education, the Common Application, ACT, and NACAC.

I wish you all the very best!

Dr. Chris

"Knowledge is Power!"

Made in the USA
San Bernardino, CA
19 December 2013